ALMONDS

EVERY WHICH WAY

ALMONDS
EVERY WHICH WAY

More than 150
Healthy & Delicious
Almond Milk, Almond Flour, and
Almond Butter Recipes

BROOKE MᶜLAY

Da Capo
LIFE
LONG

A Member of the Perseus Books Group

A Hollan Publishing, Inc. Concept
Copyright © 2014 by Brooke McLay
Photos by Brooke McLay, Franklin Bennett, and Melanie North

Editorial production by *Marra*thon Production Services. www.marrathon.net

Book design by Jane Raese
Set in 12.5-point Mrs Eaves

Library of Congress Cataloging-in-Publication Data is available for this book.

ISBN 978-0-7382-1738-3 (paper)
ISBN 978-0-7382-1739-0 (e-book)

First Da Capo Press edition 2014

Published by Da Capo Press
A Member of the Perseus Books Group
www.dacapopress.com

Note: The information in this book is true and complete to the best of our knowledge. This book is intended only as an informative guide for those wishing to know more about health issues. In no way is this book intended to replace, countermand, or conflict with the advice given to you by your own physician. The ultimate decision concerning care should be made between you and your doctor. We strongly recommend you follow his or her advice. Information in this book is general and is offered with no guarantees on the part of the authors or Da Capo Press. The authors and publisher disclaim all liability in connection with the use of this book.

Da Capo Press books are available at special discounts for bulk purchases in the U.S. by corporations, institutions, and other organizations. For more information, please contact the Special Markets Department at the Perseus Books Group, 2300 Chestnut Street, Suite 200, Philadelphia, PA, 19103, or call (800) 810-4145, ext. 5000, or e-mail special.markets@perseusbooks.com.

10 9 8 7 6 5 4 3 2 1

To Andrew, Rebecca, Jacob, and Alyssa.
You will always and for always be my favorite little tree-nuts.

CONTENTS

PREFACE

A stroll through the aisles of your local supermarket will tell you that almonds and the products derived from them have reached an all-time high in popularity. A rise in almond-based products can be attributed to a variety of reasons: some people have allergy and health concerns, while others are cutting back on gluten or dairy, and still others are looking for a plant-based source of protein. It's a wide array. Whatever your reason, with more and more almond-based products on the shelf, you can easily expand your recipe repertoire and find new ways to include newer, healthier food options in your diet—all using almond flour, butter, and milk. This book is true to its title, offering up *Almonds Every Which Way*—recipes you'll find relevant whether your aim is to lose weight, get healthier, adopt a gluten-free or paleo eating plan, or just be adventurous in the kitchen and find fresh ways to use up that jar of gourmet almond butter! Almond butter is for more than just spreading, almond milk for more than just drinking, and you haven't tasted a muffin until you've made it moist with freshly ground, blanched almond flour.

Each recipe has been tagged with icons to help you quickly find meals that work within your particular diet parameters. You'll find signs for dairy-free, gluten-free, grain-free, paleo, vegan, and vegetarian. These six diet approaches are highlighted because they best address the broad categories of diets that use almond products.

The recipes in this book range from classics you already love—made with almond ingredients swapped into the mix—to new recipe ideas that meld the luscious flavors and features of almond milk, almond butter, and almond flour into meals you'll want to make again and again.

Mostly, I hope this book serves as a starting point for experimentation. If you're looking for delicious recipes, you'll find them within the pages of this book. If you're looking for recipes that help you cut down on allergens, you'll discover dozens. If you want to stir that leftover almond butter into a batch of classic comfort food, we've got you covered. A little bit of everything, for a whole lot of everyone. Almonds are nice like that—they can be the happy center of a variety of diets, adding nutrients, making dishes allergen-free, and generally giving your meals a glow of goodness.

I hope you enjoy cooking with them as much as I do.

Brooke

ALMONDS

EVERY WHICH WAY

1

Welcome to the World of Almonds

Before you get cooking, let's start with the basics. In a nutshell, almonds in any form are a natural source of magnesium, potassium, and protein. Magnesium helps regulate the digestive system and maintain healthy bones, while potassium keeps the heart and nervous system properly maintained. Almonds have been linked to healthier skin, appear to lower blood sugar levels, and may possibly play a role in cancer prevention as well. The protein in almonds makes them a naturally low-carb way to bulk up recipes without bulking up your waistline, and 3.5 grams of fiber per ounce of almonds adds as much fiber to your diet as a banana.

Below, you'll find everything you ever needed to know about the health, nutrition—and flavor—benefits of almond flour, butter, and milk.

Almond Flour

You're likely expecting this section to start with some sort of healthy statistic, right? No way. The primary reason (in my mind, anyway) for adding almond flour to your meals isn't because it can help lower your cholesterol (though studies have shown a connection) or because swapping carbs for almond products has shown a 30 percent reduction in heart disease in many patients (though it has). Rather, the primary reason to start using almond flour in your cooking is because it makes foods—especially baked foods—absolutely scrumptious.

The natural oils in almond flour lend remarkable moistness to baked goods like muffins, cakes, and waffles. Expect a slightly denser final product with a kiss of natural almond flavor and a remarkable amount of tender texture without adding more butter to the mix.

Cooking and baking with almond flour is win-win in every way. It can lessen the amount of processed foods in your diet, drop carb intake without sacrifice, and work beautifully in recipes. It can be used as basic flour, it can take the place of carb-heavy bread crumbs, and it can be sprinkled over cobblers to create a completely natural, flavorful crust. Almond flour is surprisingly versatile; it can be used in everything from breakfasts to dinners. It's good raw or cooked, served hot or cold. That's something traditional wheat flour can't say for itself.

You'll find information on packaged flours you can find in stores or online on page 210; I also include easy DIY flour recipes on pages 26–27.

Almond Butter

Almond butter first hit store shelves as a replacement for peanut butter, but its versatility, nutritional benefits, and incredible flavor have turned basic almond butter into a mighty market for health lovers and gourmands alike.

Easy to swap into recipes that call for peanut butter, almond butter offers a mildly sweet, natural flavor and bakes beautifully into desserts. It's also an incredible base for pasta and noodle sauces. When you hit the entrée section on page 139, you'll see just how many ways there are to add almond butter into everyday cooking.

Almond butter is also good for you. Peanuts are actually considered a legume, so peanut butter contains a high percentage of lectin, which may contribute to stripping away the mucous membrane of the small intestine, and potentially increasing susceptibility to autoimmune diseases. Almond butter, as part of general almond consumption, has been linked to a lowered risk of heart disease and has high levels of the antioxidant vitamin E, which has been linked to lowered rates of cell damage.

When comparing almond butter to peanut butter, there are other nutritional benefits, as well. Almond butter is higher in magnesium and iron, both vital minerals that contribute to the well-being of nervous function and healthy skin and tissue.

Some paleo eaters may be concerned about the ratio of omega-6 to omega-3 fatty acids in almonds, because almonds are high in pro-inflammatory omega-6s. If this ratio is of concern to you, keep in mind that raw almonds, when enjoyed in recommended serving-size amounts, offer tremendous benefits without inciting a high amount of inflammation. When consumed in excess, or used as a primary source of protein, almond butter and other whole-nut almond products may increase inflammation, but in moderate amounts, the benefits of the nuts themselves far exceed any harm from the omega-6s. Almond butter is a wonderful addition to any healthy eating plan and an especially good substitute for those with peanut allergies.

You'll find information on prepackaged butters you can find in stores on pages 207–210; I also include easy DIY almond butter recipes on pages 22–25.

Almond Milk

If you're trying to avoid dairy and soy's not your first choice, almond milk is a great alternative. There are a variety of companies, flavors, and ways to store almond milk, and it easily substitutes for cow's milk in most recipes.

There are dozens of reasons almond milk is worth adding to your diet. The first is that the light, nutty, crisp flavor is almost immediately palatable. Many milk substitutes take some getting used to, but almond milk offers a similar consistency to milk and tastes great in all the same places—over cereal, in a cup of coffee, or served ice cold in a glass with a straw.

Like other almond products, almond milk will boost your intake of magnesium, potassium, and antioxidant vitamin E. It's also lower in calories than cow's milk, and many commercial almond milks are fortified with calcium, too.

Many varieties of store-bought almond milk are shelf-stable, requiring no refrigeration until open and ready for storage, so it's easy to keep stocked in the pantry. Of course, when making almond milk at home, always store it in the fridge to extend its shelf life.

Perhaps one of the best things about almond milk is how compatible it is with nearly every type of diet. Vegan, vegetarian, peanut-free, gluten-free, lactose intolerant, and paleo eaters can all enjoy almond milk. It has all the creamy goodness of milk, without all of the adverse reactions some bodies experience when consuming dairy.

You'll find information on packaged milks you can find in stores on pages 210–211. While store-bought almond milks contain some additives, it's easy to make a pure, preservative-free version of almond milk in your own kitchen. Several recipes for homemade almond milk are included in chapter 2 of this book (see pages 17–21). Homemade almond milk isn't just a clean, whole food, it's also a waste-free recipe. When making almond milk, you'll blend fresh almonds into water, drain the liquid for drinking, and be left with a pureed pith, which can be baked into cookie bars, added to quick breads (see page 16), and stirred into oatmeal, so no part of the almond goes to waste.

Tips and Tricks

How do you store almond butter? How long can almond milk last on the shelf? How much almond flour can you substitute in regular recipes? This section will share all the details for making the most of your almond ingredients.

Almond Flour

Blanched almond flour is technically a raw product and therefore requires special treatment to extend its shelf life, protect its nutrients, and keep it from going rancid. Almond flour is different from almond meal. Blanched almond flour is made by boiling or steaming the skins off almonds, then grinding them into fine particles. Almond meal is usually ground from almonds with the skins still on and tends to have a texture closer to cornmeal. For most of the recipes in this book, you'll want to use a finely ground almond flour, rather than almond meal.

Storing
Almond flour will go rancid more quickly than glutinous flours, so it's not recommended that you keep it on the shelf. Store almond flour in airtight bags or mason jars, and it will keep in the fridge for up to six months and in the freezer for up to a year. If you freeze your almond flour, it will need to be brought to room temperature before using it in recipes.

Shelf Life
3–6 months if stored in the fridge
  1 year if stored in the freezer

Pantry Tips
Buy in bulk for the best price, but immediately portion out your almond flour. Store in half-gallon or gallon-size mason jars. Keep one in the fridge for cooking and the rest in the freezer.

Almond Milk

Almond milk doesn't have the same storage requirements as cow's milk, but there are some tips for extending the shelf life of your almond milk, keeping it safe, and keeping it fresh. Homemade almond milk has different requirements from store-bought, refrigerated almond milk brands. However, a few basic practices will keep any almond milk fresher longer.

Storing
Store unopened almond milk based on the recommendations of the manufacturer. Some products are shelf-stable, others require refrigeration. When storing unopened, shelf-stable almond milk, keep it in a cool, dry location for best results. Extreme heat can adversely affect the texture of the product.

Opened almond milk should always be stored covered in the refrigerator. Store-bought brands will print an expiration date on the top of the carton; shelf-stable brands will typically encourage you to consume the milk within 7 days of opening.

Homemade almond milk should always be stored in an airtight container in the refrigerator. It may separate once stored, so give it a nice shake before opening. Because there are no additives or preservatives, homemade almond milk won't last as long as store-bought brands.

Shelf Life

Unopened, shelf-stable almond milk can typically be stored in a cool, dry location for up to 6 months. Check the packaging to ensure the safe storage date.

Opened, most store-bought almond milks will stay fresh for about 7 days under refrigeration and possibly longer, but always check the smell, taste, and texture of the milk before consuming or cooking.

Homemade almond milk should be stored covered in the fridge, and consumed in 3–5 days.

Almond Butter

Most store-bought almond butters can be stored on the shelf once opened, making them a great addition to any pantry. Here are a few important considerations for keeping your almond butter fresh, smooth, and delicious for many weeks or even months after opening.

Storing

Store unopened almond butter in a cool, dry cupboard or pantry. Many almond butter brands will have some separation of oil and nut meat, but heat will increase that separation. Heat can also speed up the aging process and make your almond butter go rancid before you've had time to use it. This is especially true of raw almond butter, so proper storage isn't just good for you—it's good for your almond butter.

No-stir brands are especially fit for shelf storage; they'll be soft and easily spreadable the moment you want to spoon into them. Storing almond butter in the fridge will extend the shelf life; however, the cool temperatures significantly thicken the texture and make it hard to spoon into or spread.

Shelf Life

Once opened, use almond butter before the expiration date to ensure freshness. Homemade nut butters should be tightly covered and can be stored in a cool, dry location for 1–2 weeks and in the fridge for up to 3 months. Almond butters—especially raw ones—can go rancid, so always smell the product before use. Rancid nut butter will give off an unsavory smell and should be discarded.

Pantry Tips

Wipe the rim of your almond butter jar clean after each use to ensure a tight seal for storage.

Use a clean knife every time you scoop into your almond butter. This keeps it from becoming contaminated with other ingredients.

For almond butters that require stirring, here's a fun trick: the first time you open the jar, use a knife to stir the oil into the nut meat. Replace the lid and store the jar upside down in the fridge for maximum freshness and less separation. It should not be stored in the freezer.

Substituting Almond Ingredients for Conventional Ingredients

Ready to replace your traditional wheat flour and dairy milk recipes with pure, natural almond products? Here's the 411 on how to make the swap.

Almond Flour

Almond flour can typically be swapped straight across for wheat flour in most baking or quick bread recipes, but keep these considerations in mind:

- **Use Finely Ground Almond Flour.** Very finely ground almond flour most mimics traditional wheat flour and will always give you the best

results. Almond meal or coarse-ground almond flour will yield crumbly baked treats that don't hold together as nicely as treats made with finely ground almond flour.

- **Bulk Up the Baking Powder.** Add an extra ½ teaspoon of baking powder per cup of almond flour added to your recipe. It will give an extra boost to the naturally heavier almond flour.

- **Cut the Fat.** Almond flour contains natural oils, so you can reduce the amount of butter or oil in your recipes by 2 tablespoons for every cup of almond flour that you add to the recipe.

- **Quick over Slow.** Quick breads, cupcakes, and muffin recipes are ideal for straight-across substitution of wheat with almond flour. Unfortunately, yeast bread recipes don't work well with a cup-for-cup swap. If you've got your heart set on foccacia, dinner rolls, or grandma's French bread recipe, try using the **ALL-PURPOSE GLUTEN-FREE ALMOND FLOUR MIX (PAGE 27).**

- **Don't Expect Perfection.** Cooking with almond flour is different from cooking with wheat flour. So the results of any recipe will be slightly different from the original. Wheat flour tends to rise higher than almond flour recipes. When made with almond flour, most recipes will be denser and slightly more crumbly than they would be if made from wheat flour. However, the flavor of many recipes is greatly enhanced when almond flour is swapped in, and the low-carb benefits far outweigh the texture difference!

Almond Milk

Almond milk can be used in a most recipes calling for cow's milk or soy milk. It's easy to make a cup-for-cup swap in soups, sauces, baked goods, even drinks, milkshakes, and smoothies. When adding almond milk to savory sauces, unsweetened almond milk is always best. The flavor and texture of the finished recipe may be slightly thinner than cow's milk and will have the addition of mild almond flavor, versus the creamy flavor of cow's milk.

- **Use It in Pudding.** Most almond milk companies don't recommend using almond milk in instant pudding. Here's a secret: add 2 teaspoons of cornstarch to a small package of instant pudding and whisk in 1 ½ cups of almond milk. Presto! Perfect pudding every time.
- **Keep It Sweet.** When making sweet sauces or baked goods, feel free to swap sweetened vanilla almond milk in place of cow's milk. The sugar content in your recipe can be cut by 1 tablespoon per ½ cup of sweetened almond milk added.

- **Skinny Secrets.** Unsweetened almond milk typically cooks and bakes like skim milk. For thicker, creamier sauces, try bulking up the cream content of your recipe by adding ¼ cup of full-fat coconut milk to unsweetened almond milk for a rich, thick final dish.

Almond Butter

Almond butter is the easiest swap of them all! Use it cup for cup in recipes calling for peanut butter. The only thing to keep in mind: make sure you've stirred your almond butter well—or use a no-stir brand—for best results.

How to Make the Recipes in This Book Work for You— Special Tips for Special Diets

The recipes in this book highlight the healthy aspects of swapping almond products for some of the traditional ingredients that more and more diets are trying to avoid. Paleo eaters avoid flour. Vegans eschew any form of animal product, including eggs and dairy milk. Vegetarians want protein without eating meat. And gluten-free and grain-free dieters need zero gluten in their dishes. For each of these diet approaches, almonds make delicious substitutes. From acting like flour to baking as a filler in Vegan Meatloaf, almond products can help you abide by your dietary restrictions in delicious ways. In the recipes, I've noted where specific types of almond milk or almond butter are needed. Otherwise, feel free to use whatever is in your pantry or fridge.

The recipes in this book have been marked with diet icons, making it easy for you to quickly identify which recipes fit into your preferred eating plan:

- **D** Dairy-free
- **gL** Gluten-free
- **gR** Grain-free
- **pL** Paleo (Strict paleo eaters will want to avoid canned foods, but we've included pure versions.)
- **PN** Peanut
- **VE** Vegan
- **VT** Vegetarian

Note that each recipe includes an icon for every possible diet type it fits or can be tailored to fit, using ingredient substitutions, which are also included.

» » »

Many of the recipes contain ingredient swaps. Here's a quick guide to help you see which swap is right for you when several options are offered for a single ingredient in a recipe.

Flavor Enhancers

Soy sauce, tamari, and Bragg Liquid Aminos give a salty, smoky flavor to rec-

ipes, but contain very different ingredients. Traditional soy sauce is often filled with gluten, so check the ingredients before adding if you're a g-free eater. Tamari is typically made without wheat (again, check the label to be safe), and many paleo and vegan eaters approve this as an acceptable alternative to soy sauce. Bragg Liquid Aminos are likewise made out of soybeans but are not fermented and contain no gluten. For strict non-soy eaters, coconut aminos can also be added to these recipes for a similar flavor and consistency. Here, then, is a quick recap:

Soy sauce—vegetarian, vegan (but check label), paleo
Tamari—gluten-free, grain-free, vegetarian, vegan, paleo
Bragg Liquid Aminos—gluten-free, grain-free, vegetarian, vegan, paleo
Coconut aminos—gluten-free, grain-free, vegetarian, vegan, paleo

Oils

Three different oils are mentioned interchangeably in several of the recipes in this book. Grapeseed, avocado, and olive oil are easy to find in most grocers and yield almost identical results in recipes. More attention is being given to the smoking point of olive oil. It's not recommended for use in hot skillets or stir-frys because it smokes at a low point and can release potentially harmful free radicals. Of these oils, avocado oil has the highest smoking point (at 520°F) and is safest to use for stir-frying and baking. Grapeseed and olive oil are best for drizzling but can be used for cooking in a pinch. Here's the lowdown on which oil will work best for your diet:

Grapeseed oil—gluten-free, grain-free, vegetarian, vegan

Avocado—gluten-free, grain-free, vegetarian, vegan, paleo

Olive—gluten-free, grain-free, vegetarian, vegan, paleo

Fats

When it comes to baking and sautéing, nothing lends as much flavor as butter! But, butter can be a big no-no for some of our special diets. So you'll see several recipes that offer alternative options. Followers of the paleo diet, in particular, will want to use grass-fed butter. Vegans will prefer a butter-like spread such as Earth Balance. And all diet types can enjoy coconut oil, which bakes just like butter in most recipes but can lend a coconut flavor that some eaters simply don't enjoy. No worries. I've listed plenty of swap options for the fats in the recipes. Here is a summary of which fats work best with which diets:

Butter—gluten-free, grain-free, vegetarian

Grass-fed butter—gluten-free, grain-free, vegetarian, paleo

Earth Balance—gluten-free, grain-free, vegetarian, vegan

Coconut oil—gluten-free, grain-free, vegetarian, vegan, paleo

Sugars

Healthy eating often means cutting down on sugar and sweeteners that can spike your blood sugar. Many of the recipes in this book were developed with a low-sugar approach. You'll find tons of flavor, just enough sweetness, and a variety of options for making your dishes happy for your eating type. Here's a list of the sweeteners listed interchangeably in this book, and the diets that use them:

Pure maple syrup—dairy-free, gluten-free, grain-free, paleo, vegetarian, vegan

Agave nectar—dairy-free, gluten-free, grain-free, vegetarian, vegan

Raw honey—dairy-free, gluten-free, grain-free, vegetarian

Brown sugar—dairy-free, gluten-free, grain-free, vegetarian, vegan

Stevia—dairy-free, gluten-free, grain-free, paleo (not recommended except for drink recipes), vegetarian, vegan

Sucanat—dairy-free, gluten-free, grain-free, paleo (strict paleo eaters will avoid all sugars), vegetarian, vegan

Thickening Agents

Where flour was once used as a thickener in gravies, sauces, soups, and custards, cornstarch can be swapped in. But what if you're avoiding corn products, or trying to cut carbs with a paleo diet? Arrowroot powder, made from the starchy arrowroot plant, offers a great alternative. It's called for in many recipes in this book. It works very similarly to cornstarch, but thickens before the boiling point is reached (and if it passes the boiling point, it turns into a gloppy mess). If you don't have arrowroot powder in your kitchen and don't mind cooking with cornstarch, feel free to boost the amount of cornstarch by 1 teaspoon per tablespoon of arrowroot powder and your recipes should turn out splendidly! Here is a quick guide to thickening agents and their suitability to various diets:

    Arrowroot powder—gluten-free,
        grain-free, vegetarian, vegan, paleo
    Cornstarch—gluten-free, vegetarian,
        vegan
    Flaxseed meal—gluten-free, grain-
        free, vegetarian, vegan

Salt

Sea salt is called for in most recipes in this book, but I secretly prefer using Himalayan pink salt or crystallized salt flakes when I cook. They're almost sensual versions of plain old table salt and lend beautiful texture to final dishes. Feel free to use your favorite unflavored salt. The amounts in the recipes are minimums, good starting points for most eaters, but you can always add extra salt if you prefer. Unless specified, it's not recommended that coarse sea salt or coarse kosher salt be used in recipes, because many recipes don't allow sufficient time to dissolve the large salt crystals into their batters or doughs.

Nutritional Values

The nutritional values have been calculated and included for all 151 dishes and follow the directions of each recipe. The amounts given have been calculated per serving size. Keep in mind the numbers are estimates only, and for recipes that list alternative ingredients, the numbers are based on the first ingredient listed. The percentages included in the nutrition lists are based on the FDA-approved daily values for a 2,000-calorie-per-day diet for adults. When alternate ingredients are used, nutritional content will change. To check the measurements of your recipe with ingredient swaps, you can access the same online tools used to calculate the original nutritional numbers at:

    http://www.saymmm.com/grocerylist.
    php

http://caloriecount.about.com/cc/
recipe_analysis.php

Where variations are given, the recipe is marked as Paleo or Vegan or Gluten-free.

Kitchen Essentials

With a focus on healthy eating, several of the recipes in this book call for special equipment. In recipes where specific prep tools are called for, I've tried to offer alternate suggestions, just in case you're cooking in a kitchen with limited storage space and even more limited access to haute kitchenware. That said, there are a few kitchen tools worth keeping around. These items make recipe prep a snap and are specifically called for in the directions section for many recipes in this book.

Cheesecloth. Cheesecloth can be found in the kitchen goods section of some grocery stores, but is easiest to find online. Use cheesecloth for very fine straining— you'll see it called for in the homemade almond milk recipes in this book. Once you've used cheesecloth, discard it. The fine weaving of the cloth doesn't stand up well to washing machines.

Stand Mixer. An electric hand-held mixer can be used if you don't have a stand mixer, but a high-speed, no-hands-needed stand mixer makes baking and beating easier than ever.

High-Speed, Industrial-Strength Blender. Vitamix and Blendtec blenders have become favorite tools for many home chefs because of their versatility. Powerful enough to puree nut butter, fast enough to heat soups and sauces as they blend, a high-speed blender offers dramatically different results than a traditional blender. Recipes calling for a high-speed blender typically offer alternate prep ideas, in case you're still working with a traditional blender. A limited number of recipes in this book require a high-speed blender for best results. Be sure to check the directions of any recipe before starting, to ensure you have the proper equipment in your kitchen. For smoothies and sauces, a conventional blender will work just fine.

Hand-held Blender. For quick pureeing of soups, sauces, smoothies, and frothy drinks, hand-held blenders are great to have around! They typically cost less than $25, making them an inexpensive tool to keep in the kitchen.

Large Food Processor. Large food processors are called for in several recipes in this book and really come in handy when making homemade almond butter and almond flour. Though smaller, less-expensive food processors are available, the large food processors are more powerful and yield a finer texture and faster results than their smaller counterparts.

Donut Pan. Available in specialty kitchen stores and in the baking aisle of some big-box chains, donut pans make it easy to bake donuts and keep your kitchen free of fried foods. Most muffin recipes can be baked in donut pans, making them more useable than you might think when you first consider springing for a donut pan of your own. If you don't have a donut pan, a mini muffin tin will turn baked donut dough into mini "doughnut holes"—just remember to check mini muffins for doneness at around 8–10 minutes.

Parchment-lined baking sheets and bakeware are specified in most recipes in this book. If you don't have parchment, nonstick cooking spray will work. But, prepping your bakeware with parchment (though slightly more time-consuming than dousing your pan with a quick spray of nonstick) is worth it. Parchment paper contains no preservatives and adds zero calories. You can quickly cut it to the size you need. It also protects your bakeware and makes for easy clean-up.

Pantry Prep: Ingredients to Have on Hand

Here are the ingredients called for most often in this cookbook. Keep them in your pantry and fridge for extra-quick mealtime prep.

Almond Products

Finely-ground, blanched almond flour
Raw almond butter
Raw maple almond butter
Roasted almond butter, creamy
Unsweetened almond milk
Vanilla—sweetened or unsweetened—almond milk

Oils

Avocado, olive, or grapeseed oil
Coconut oil
Mongolian Fire Oil (available in the Asian section of most grocery stores)
Sesame oil or toasted sesame oil

Spices and Seasonings

Apple pie spice
Cayenne
Cinnamon
Curry powder
Ginger
Italian seasoning
Peppercorns

Pumpkin pie spice
Pure almond extract
Pure vanilla extract
Salt
Vanilla bean

Sweeteners

Honey
Maple syrup
Powdered sugar
Sugar

Nuts and Seeds

Flaxseed meal
Raw almonds
Raw cashews
Sesame seeds

Dry Goods

Arrowroot powder or cornstarch
Baking powder
Brown rice flour
Cocoa powder
Coconut flour
Flour or gluten-free flour mix
Potato starch
Quick oats
Sorghum

Sauces and Stock

Chicken or vegetable stock
Green curry paste

Soy sauce
Sriracha

Other

Coconut milk (full-fat recommended)
Nutritional yeast (available online or at
    most natural food grocers)
Vegan chocolate chips

Meat and Dairy

The recipes in this cookbook have been created with large, organic eggs in mind. In keeping with our focus on healthy food options, it's strongly recommended that grass-fed meat and dairy products be your choice at the grocery store; organic meats and dairy products are second best; and conventionally raised meat and dairy are acceptable, but not preferred.

Bacon
Eggs
Chicken
Ground beef
Steak

Fruits

Fresh produce is preferred for ingredients when preparing each of the recipes for this book, unless otherwise noted. However, frozen produce can be used in a pinch and no-salt-added canned fruit or veggies can be used as a substitute.

Fruit

Apples
Blackberries
Blueberries
Dates
Lemons
Limes
Pears
Pumpkins
Raspberries
Strawberries
Tomatoes

Veggies

Basil
Carrots
Garlic
Jalapeño
Onions
Potatoes
Scallions
Shallots
Squash

2

Homemade Basics

Although packaged almond ingredients are readily available and are a great convenience, you don't have to pay big bucks. Almond basics are surprisingly simple to make and are often more suited for baking and cooking than the packaged products (kiss those preservative-laden bottles and packages goodbye). Almond milk is more pure when made from scratch, almond butter creamier. And you yourself can grind almond flour finer and for significantly fewer pennies than the most accessible brands on the shelves.

Almond milks, butters, and flours that come in a variety of flavors are all so simple to make yourself. Here are all the tips, tricks, and techniques to get you started.

USE THAT LEFTOVER ALMOND PULP!

When making your own almond milk, you'll have lots of leftover almond pulp. Don't throw that stuff away! It's wonderful to add to recipes, bulking up the protein content and lending lots of gorgeous almond flavor. Here are a few ways to store and use leftover almond pulp.

» **Bake with It.** Replace up to one cup of flour or almond flour with almond pulp in brownie, cookie, or quick bread recipes.

» **Puree It.** Add several tablespoons of pulp to hummus and pump up the protein in your favorite dips.

» **Blend It.** Put a tablespoon of almond pulp in your smoothies for extra protein and a heartier texture.

» **Store It.** Place wet almond pulp in an airtight container and keep it in the fridge for up to two weeks.

» **Dry It.** Spread wet almond pulp on a parchment-lined baking sheet and place in an oven heated to 225°F. Stir with a spatula as needed until dried. Store in an airtight container in the fridge, and use in recipes calling for almond flour.

Unsweetened Almond Milk

Making your own almond milk is surprisingly simple. The process requires a little prep (overnight soaking of the almonds) and a slightly untraditional kitchen pantry item (cheesecloth), but is otherwise an easy way to create a preservative-free almond milk right at home.

1 cup raw almonds
4 cups filtered water
Pinch of sea salt

1. Place the almonds in a large bowl. Cover with water and soak them overnight.
2. Rinse and drain sthe oaked almonds and place them in a high-speed blender or food processor along with the filtered water and salt. Blend on high for 60 seconds, then place a piece of cheesecloth in a strainer over a large bowl (cut the cheesecloth large enough to rest in the bowl with several inches left over the edges of the bowl).
3. Pour the contents of the blender into the cheesecloth. Fold up the edges of the cheesecloth and gently squeeze the cheesecloth to release the milk.
4. Pour into a large jar or pitcher with an airtight seal. Store in the refrigerator for 3–5 days. Shake the jar before serving.

Note: Nut milk bags are available from a variety of online retailers and can be used in place of the cheesecloth.

TIP: Need almond milk in a pinch? Soak the almonds in hot water for 1–2 hours to speed the preparation process.

(D) (gL) (pL) (vE) (vT)

MAKES 8 SERVINGS

PER SERVING (⅛ RECIPE)

Calories: 103
Calories from Fat: 68
Total Fat: 9g, 14%
Saturated Fat: 1g, 5%
Total Carb: 4g, 1%
Dietary Fiber: 2g, 8%
Sugars: 1g
Protein: 4g
Cholesterol: 0mg, 0%
Sodium: 242mg, 10%

Vanilla Almond Milk

This slightly sweet, vanilla-kissed milk is perfect for drinking cold right out the fridge or for pouring over a bowl of cereal. Add a pinch of cinnamon for a horchata-esque flavor.

D
gL
nL
vE
vT

1 cup raw almonds
4 cups filtered water
3 tablespoons maple syrup
Seeds of ½ vanilla bean
Pinch of sea salt

MAKES 8 SERVINGS

**PER SERVING
(⅛ RECIPE)**

Calories: 131
Calories from Fat: 88
Total Fat: 10g, 15%
Saturated Fat: 1g, 5%
Total Carb: 8g, 3%
Dietary Fiber: 2g, 8%
Sugars: 4g
Protein: 4g
Cholesterol: 0mg, 0%
Sodium: 243mg, 10%

1. Place the almonds in a large bowl. Cover with water and soak them overnight.
2. Rinse and drain the soaked almonds and place them in a high-speed blender or food processor along with the filtered water. Blend on high for 60 seconds, then place a piece of cheesecloth in a strainer over a large bowl (cut the cheesecloth large enough to rest in the bowl with several inches left over the edges of the bowl).
3. Pour the contents of the blender into the cheesecloth. Fold up the edges of the cheesecloth and gently squeeze the cheesecloth to release the milk.
4. Place the almond milk back in the blender and add the maple syrup, vanilla bean seeds, and salt. Blend until frothy.
5. Pour into a large jar or pitcher with an airtight seal. Store in the refrigerator for 3–5 days. Shake the jar before serving.

Note: Nut milk bags are available from a variety of online retailers and can be used in place of the cheesecloth.

TIP: Need almond milk in a pinch? Soak the almonds in hot water for 1–2 hours to speed the preparation process.

Coconut Almond Milk

Creamy and rich, Coconut Almond Milk tastes great served over desserts or whisked into Indian-inspired sauces. The coconut milk makes it high in calories and fat content, but it's also high in satiety. Try heating a cup of it with 2 tablespoons of raw butter and 2 ounces of rum for a comforting hot toddy on a winter evening.

1 cup raw almonds

4 cups unsweetened coconut water

1 (13.66-ounce) can coconut milk

2 tablespoons maple syrup

1 tablespoon pure vanilla extract

1. Place the almonds a large bowl and cover with the coconut water. Soak overnight.
2. Rinse and drain the soaked almonds and place them in a blender (regular or high-speed will work). Blend on high for 60 seconds, then place a piece of cheesecloth in a strainer over a large bowl (cut the cheesecloth large enough to rest in the bowl with several inches left over the edges of the bowl).
3. Pour the contents of the blender into the cheesecloth. Fold up the edges of the cheesecloth and squeeze the cheesecloth to remove the milk.
4. Place the almond milk back in the blender and add the coconut milk, maple syrup, and vanilla. Blend until frothy.
5. Pour into a large jar or pitcher with an airtight seal. Store in the fridge for 3–5 days. Shake the jar before serving.

Note: Nut milk bags are available from a variety of online retailers and can be used in place of the cheesecloth.

TIP: Need almond milk in a pinch? Soak the almonds in hot water for 1–2 hours to speed the preparation process.

MAKES 8 SERVINGS

PER SERVING (⅛ RECIPE)

Calories: 234

Calories from Fat: 197

Total Fat: 19g, 29%

Saturated Fat: 10g, 50%

Total Carb: 12g, 4%

Dietary Fiber: 3g, 12%

Sugars: 6g

Protein: 6g

Cholesterol: 0mg, 0%

Sodium: 126mg, 5%

Chocolate Almond Milk

Indulge your chocolate cravings! Unsweetened cocoa and maple syrup blend to make a perfectly balanced flavor, without adding tons of calories. If you're eating paleo, substitute raw honey for the maple syrup or omit it altogether for a less sweet treat.

D
GL
pL
VE
VT

1 batch **VANILLA ALMOND MILK (PAGE 18)**

3 tablespoons cocoa powder

2 tablespoons maple syrup

1. Place all the ingredients in a blender. Blend until frothy.
2. Serve immediately or pour it into a large jar or pitcher with an airtight seal. Store in the refrigerator for 3–5 days. Shake the jar before serving.

Note: Nut milk bags are available from a variety of online retailers and can be used in place of the cheesecloth.

TIP: Need almond milk in a pinch? Soak the almonds in hot water for 1–2 hours to speed the preparation process.

MAKES 8 SERVINGS

**PER SERVING
(⅛ RECIPE)**

Calories: 145

Calories from Fat: 25

Total Fat: 10g, 15%

Saturated Fat: 1g, 5%

Total Carb: 11g, 4%

Dietary Fiber: 3g 12%

Sugars: 6g

Protein: 5g

Cholesterol: 0mg, 0%

Sodium: 244mg, 10%

Cashew Almond Milk

Cashews lend a natural sweetness, which offsets the mild flavor of almond in this simple recipe. Because the cashew fats emulsify, the texture of this milk will be slightly thicker than traditional almond milk, making it a perfect addition to milkshakes and smoothies.

½ cup raw almonds
⅔ cup raw cashews
4 cups filtered water
1 tablespoon pure vanilla extract

1. Place the almonds and cashews in a large bowl and cover them with water. Soak them overnight.
2. Rinse and drain s the oaked nuts and place them in a blender (regular or high-speed will work) with the filtered water and vanilla. Blend on high for 60 seconds, then place a piece of cheesecloth in a strainer over a large bowl (cut the cheesecloth large enough to rest in the bowl with several inches left over the edges of the bowl).
3. Pour the contents of the blender into the cheesecloth. Fold up the edges of the cheesecloth and squeeze the cheesecloth to remove the milk.
4. Place the nut milk back in the blender. Blend until frothy.
5. Pour into a large jar or pitcher with an airtight seal. Store in the fridge for 3–5 days. Shake the jar before serving.

Note: Nut milk bags are available from a variety of online retailers and can be used in place of the cheesecloth.

TIP: Need almond milk in a pinch? Soak the almonds in hot water for 1–2 hours to speed the preparation process.

D
gL
pL
vE
vT

MAKES 8 SERVINGS

**PER SERVING
(⅛ RECIPE)**

Calories: 177
Calories from Fat: 104
Total Fat: 14g, 22%
Saturated Fat: 2g, 10%
Total Carb: 8g, 3%
Dietary Fiber: 3g, 12%
Sugars: 2g
Protein: 6g
Cholesterol: 0mg 0%
Sodium: 77mg, 3%

Bare-Bones Raw Almond Butter

Here's your most basic almond butter, not an ounce of processed anything added to it. As you make this in your food processor, you'll see it go through a variety of stages—from chunky to sand-like clumps. It takes a while to get to the creamy butter phase, nearly 15 minutes. But the end result is a surprisingly creamy, naturally sweet almond butter, which costs a lot less than the stuff you buy in the store! This recipe can also be made in an industrial-strength blender. Follow the manufacturer's instructions on making nut butters for best results.

2 cups raw almonds

½ teaspoon sea salt (optional)

1. Place the almonds in a large food processor. Pulse until the almonds begin to look sandy (about 1–2 minutes), then let the food processor run for 10–15 minutes, scraping down the sides as necessary. As the almonds process, the oils will release and create a creamy butter. Add the salt, if including.
2. Store in an airtight container for up to 1 week on the shelf, and 2 weeks in the fridge.

Home-Roasted Almond Butter

1. Preheat the oven to 350°F.
2. Place 2 cups raw almonds on a parchment-lined baking sheet and roast in the oven for 10–12 minutes, turning the sheet once in the middle of the baking time.
3. Allow the almonds to cool before placing them in a large food processor.
4. Add the salt, if including.
5. Pulse until the almonds begin to look sandy (1–2 minutes), then let the food processor run for 10–15 minutes, scraping down the sides as necessary. As the almonds process, the oils will release and create a creamy butter.

D
GL
DL
VE
VT

MAKES 16 SERVINGS

PER SERVING (1 TABLESPOON)

Servings: 16

Calories: 137

Calories from Fat: 106

Total Fat: 11.7g, 14%

Saturated Fat: 0.9g, 5%

Total Carb: 4g, 1%

Dietary Fiber: 2g, 8%

Sugars: 1g

Protein: 4g

Cholesterol: 0mg, 0%

Sodium: 0mg, 0%

Chocolate Almond Butter

Creamy chocolate has never tasted better! Delicious when spread on toast or a surprising dip for fruit and cookies, this Chocolate Almond Butter is a perfect pantry item, one of those must-have recipes so snacks-on-the-go are easy, healthy, and ready when you are.

2 cups raw almonds

3 tablespoons raw honey

⅓ cup unsweetened cocoa powder

½ teaspoon sea salt

1. Preheat the oven to 350°F.
2. Place the almonds on a parchment-lined baking sheet and roast in the oven for 10–12 minutes, turning the sheet once in the middle of the baking time.
3. Allow the almonds to cool before placing them in a large food processor.
4. Pulse until the almonds begin to look sandy (1–2 minutes), then let the food processor run for 10–15 minutes, scraping down the sides as necessary. As the almonds process, the oils will release and create a creamy butter.
5. Once the preferred consistency is reached, add the honey, cocoa powder, and sea salt. Pulse until all the ingredients are well mixed.

MAKES 16 SERVINGS

PER SERVING (1 TABLESPOON)

Calories: 119

Calories from Fat: 84

Total Fat: 9g, 14%

Saturated Fat: 1g, 5%

Total Carb: 8g, 3%

Dietary Fiber: 3g, 12%

Sugars: 4g

Protein: 4g

Cholesterol: 0mg, 0%

Sodium: 73mg, 3%

Honeyed Vanilla Almond Butter

Raw honey pairs perfectly with roasted almonds in this creamy almond butter. For extra creaminess and a beautiful, buttery spread for rolls and toast, add 2 tablespoons of real butter or coconut oil to this recipe. You'll want to store that version in the fridge, but you'll love how well it spreads on hot, toasty bread!

2 cups raw almonds

4 tablespoons raw honey

½ teaspoon salt

Seeds from 1 vanilla bean or ½ tablespoon pure vanilla extract

1. Preheat the oven to 350°F.
2. Place the almonds on a parchment-lined baking sheet and roast in the oven for 10–12 minutes, turning the sheet once in the middle of the baking time.
3. Allow the almonds to cool before placing them in a large food processor.
4. Pulse until the almonds begin to look sandy (1–2 minutes), then let the food processor run for 10–15 minutes, scraping down the sides as necessary. As the almonds process, the oils will release and create a creamy butter.
5. Once the desired consistency is reached, add the honey, salt, and vanilla seeds. Process until all the ingredients are well mixed.

D
gL
gR
nb
VE
VT

MAKES 16 SERVINGS

PER SERVING (1 TABLESPOON)

Calories: 119

Calories from Fat: 84

Total Fat: 9g, 14%

Saturated Fat: 1g, 5%

Total Carb: 8g, 3%

Dietary Fiber: 2g, 8%

Sugars: 5g

Protein: 4g

Cholesterol: 0mg, 0%

Sodium: 73mg, 3%

Go Gourmet!

Turn your homemade Honeyed Vanilla Almond Butter into a gourmet-inspired spread. Here are a few favorite flavor variations on the vanilla version:

Cinnamon-Almond Butter: Add 1 teaspoon cinnamon to the almond butter before blending.

Maple-Vanilla Almond Butter: Use pure maple syrup, instead of honey, to sweeten your almond butter. Add ¼ teaspoon maple extract before blending to boost the flavor.

Salted Caramel Almond Butter: Blend your almond butter with ⅓ cup brown sugar and 3 tablespoons sweetened condensed milk instead of honey.

Basic Almond Flour

It's easy to make your own almond flour, though blanching (aka removing the almond skins) may sound like a new and overwhelming task. Fear not. It's surprisingly easy. In fact, it's so easy, you can blanch an entire batch of almonds in about a minute. Really! One minute. This recipe walks you through the basics of blanching almonds, then shows you how to blend them into a soft, smooth homemade almond flour. Blanching the almonds gives your almond flour a smooth texture and even color and allows you to purchase the less-expensive bulk bags of raw almonds, making it more affordable than ever to cook with almond flour.

2 cups raw almonds

1. To blanch almonds: place them in a pot of boiling water. Let them boil for exactly 60 seconds, then drain them immediately in a colander.
2. Run cold water over the almonds, then turn them out on a clean towel and gently dry them.
3. The almond skins will be shriveled and easy to remove. Simply press an almond between your fingers and pull off the skin.
4. Once all the almonds are blanched, place them in a large food processor and pulse them until very finely ground.
5. Store almond flour in an airtight container in the fridge for up to 6 months.

D **GL** **GR** **PL** **VE** **VT**

MAKES 3 CUPS

PER SERVING (PER ¼ CUP)

Calories: 206
Calories from Fat: 136
Total Fat: 18g, 28%
Saturated Fat: 1g, 5%
Total Carb: 8g, 3%
Dietary Fiber: 4g, 16%
Sugars: 1g
Protein: 8g
Cholesterol: 0mg, 0%
Sodium: 0mg, 0%

All-Purpose Gluten-Free Almond Flour Mix

This recipe works well as a cup-for-cup substitute for most ingredients calling for traditional white flour. Mix several batches of this flour ahead of time, keep it stored in an airtight container in your fridge, and you'll have it ready to mix into any of the recipes that call for wheat flour in this book, or try it in your favorite family dishes.

1 cup sorghum or brown rice flour

1 cup potato starch or cornstarch

½ cup finely ground, blanched almond flour

1 teaspoon xanthan gum

1. Combine all the ingredients in a large bowl.
2. Store the flour covered in a cool, dry place for up to 1 month. Store in an airtight container in the fridge for the longest storage life.

MAKES 2½ CUPS

PER SERVING (PER ¼ CUP)

Calories: 88

Calories from Fat: 6

Total Fat: 1g, 2%

Saturated Fat: 0g, 0%

Total Carb: 19g, 6%

Dietary Fiber: 1g, 4%

Sugars: 0g

Protein: 3g

Cholesterol: 0mg, 0%

Sodium: 1mg, 0%

3

Breakfast

Start your mornings off right with satisfying breakfasts that span the spectrum from sweet to savory. These eighteen recipes make clever use of almond ingredients to turn your breakfast faves into healthy, wholesome meals your whole family will adore.

If you're looking for a hearty start for your day, try making the rich, flavorful Overnight Almond Butter Oats with Fresh Peaches and Cream, which cooks in your crockpot while you sleep, then meets you in the morning piping hot and perfectly sweet. For lazy Saturday mornings, greet the day with homemade almond waffles mounded high with delicious, healthy toppings. For a lighter option, try the easy McMuffin Morning Munchers for a quick and healthy twist on classic breakfast fare.

No matter what sort of recipe you're looking for, you'll be certain to find new, everyday go-to's as well as special weekend treats!

Lacy Almond Crepes

Piping-hot crepes like the ones made by street vendors in Paris are delicious, but they're also made with white flour. This version turns traditional crepes into flavorful, delicious almond flour crepes. Perfect when stuffed with fresh fruits and whipped cream, or topped with pure maple syrup, these crepes may just have you feeling like you're enjoying brunch in France!

5 eggs
½ cup blanched almond flour
1 tablespoon honey
1 tablespoon pure vanilla extract
¼ teaspoon sea salt
4 tablespoons butter or coconut oil

1. In a blender, combine the eggs, flour, honey, vanilla, and salt. Pulse until very well mixed.
2. Heat a large nonstick skillet over medium heat. For each crepe, melt a half-teaspoon of butter in the skillet, spreading the melted butter around to coat the bottom of the skillet.
3. Spoon ¼ cup of the batter into the skillet. Quickly swirl the skillet around to spread the batter very thin across the bottom of the skillet.
4. Cook the crepe just until it begins to peel back slightly around the edges, about 30–45 seconds.
5. Use a spatula to lift the crepe from the skillet. Serve with your favorite toppings. (See the Variations opposite for a few favorite ideas.)

MAKES 12 CREPES

**PER SERVING
(1 CREPE)**

Calories: 88
Calories from Fat: 51
Total Fat: 6g, 9%
Saturated Fat: 3g, 15%
Total Carb: 6g, 2%
Dietary Fiber: 0g, 0%
Sugars: 2g
Protein: 3g
Cholesterol: 78mg, 26%
Sodium: 118mg, 5%

Fresh and Healthy Ways to Stuff Your Crepes

Crepes can be a delicious breakfast or a decadent dessert. Here are some of my favorite healthy ways to stuff crepes.

> Fresh berries drizzled with honey or maple syrup

> Bananas and **CHOCOLATE ALMOND BUTTER (PAGE 23)**

> Fresh mango, banana, and toasted coconut with a drizzle of coconut milk

> Fresh spinach wilted in garlic, topped with **ALMOND MILK ALFREDO (PAGE 156)**

> Avocado slices and pico de gallo salsa

Paleo Almond Banana Pancakes

Just three ingredients are all you need for these quick-and-easy pancakes. They are surprisingly delicious for such a simple dish. Serve them with a bit of maple syrup, or top with homemade blackberry syrup, made by boiling fresh or frozen blackberries with a shot or two of maple syrup and pure vanilla extract.

3 large ripe bananas

2 eggs

4 tablespoons almond butter

1. Place all the ingredients in a blender. Blend just until combined.
2. Heat a skillet or griddle to medium heat. Spray it with nonstick cooking spray or coat it with a small amount of melted coconut oil.
3. Pour ¼ cup of the batter onto the pan. Cook the pancake until it's golden brown, about 3–4 minutes. Flip it and cook it on the other side until it's also golden brown, another 2–3 minutes. Repeat with the remaining batter. Serve immediately.

MAKES 4 SERVINGS

**PER SERVING
(1 PANCAKE)**

Calories: 209

Calories from Fat: 104

Total Fat: 10g, 15%

Saturated Fat: 1g, 5%

Total Carb: 26g, 9%

Dietary Fiber: 4g, 16%

Sugars: 13g

Protein: 7g

Cholesterol: 82mg, 27%

Sodium: 63mg, 3%

Vegan Almond Butter Pancakes

Most prepackaged biscuit mixes are vegan, but you can swap the biscuit mix in this recipe for a cup of flour, ¾ teaspoon baking powder, and a pinch of salt. White whole wheat flour will also work in this recipe, and almond flour can be added so long as you mix in ½ tablespoon of arrowroot powder as well.

FOR THE PANCAKES

1 cup biscuit mix, gluten-free if desired

¾ cup pumpkin puree

2 tablespoons almond butter

1 teaspoon pumpkin pie spice

1 teaspoon pure vanilla extract

⅔ cup almond milk

⅔ cup dairy-free chocolate chips

FOR THE BERRY SYRUP

3 tablespoons pure maple syrup

1 ½ cups frozen berry mix

MAKES 6 PANCAKES

**PER SERVING
(1 PANCAKE)**

Calories: 326

Calories from Fat: 112

Total Fat: 14g, 22%

Saturated Fat: 6g, 30%

Total Carb: 45g, 15%

Dietary Fiber: 2g, 8%

Sugars: 30g

Protein: 6g

Cholesterol: 7mg, 2%

Sodium: 252mg, 11%

1. Whisk all the pancake ingredients together in a large bowl.
2. Heat a griddle to medium heat. Spray it with nonstick cooking spray. Spoon ¼ cup of batter onto the hot griddle. Cook the pancake on one side until it's golden brown, about 2–3 minutes. Flip it and cook the second side for 1–2 minutes, until it's golden brown. Repeat with the remaining batter.
3. In a small saucepan, cook the maple syrup and berries together just until boiling. Remove from the heat and spoon the syrup over your warm pancakes.

Almond Butter Syrup

This sweet syrup is delicious drizzled over pancakes or bowls of hot oatmeal. For an extra-quick breakfast, try drizzling it over a bowl of sliced strawberries and bananas. This syrup adds a bit of sweetness, a kick of protein, and a lot of flavor.

½ cup vanilla almond milk
½ cup raw almond butter
4 tablespoons honey, agave nectar, or maple syrup
¼ teaspoon maple or almond extract

1. Place all the ingredients in a blender. Puree until they're well blended.
2. Transfer the mixture to a microwave-safe dish or small saucepan and cook it just until heated. Serve it over pancakes, waffles, or French toast.

D
gL
gR
pL
VE
VT

MAKES 8 SERVINGS

**PER SERVING
(⅛ RECIPE)**

Calories: 108
Calories from Fat: 80
Total Fat: 8g, 12%
Saturated Fat: 1g, 5%
Total Carb: 5g, 2%
Dietary Fiber: 2g, 8%
Sugars: 2g
Protein: 4g
Cholesterol: 2mg, 1%
Sodium: 48mg, 2%

Basic Berry Waffles

What is breakfast without a basic waffle recipe? This almond flour waffle is kissed with sweetness, spotted with berries, and full of protein. Be sure to spray your waffle iron with nonstick cooking spray to keep the waffles from sticking.

1 ½ cups blanched almond flour

3 tablespoons arrowroot powder

1 ½ teaspoons baking powder

½ teaspoon salt

1 tablespoon honey, agave nectar, or maple syrup

1 tablespoon coconut oil, butter, or Earth Balance, melted

⅔ cup almond milk

½ cup fresh or frozen blueberries, raspberries, or blackberries

1. In a large bowl, whisk together the almond flour, arrowroot powder, baking powder, and salt.
2. Add the honey, coconut oil, and almond milk. Whisk them together until a smooth batter forms.
3. Fold in the berries.
4. Spoon ¼ of the batter onto the waffle iron and cook until it's golden brown, about 3–4 minutes. Repeat with the remaining batter.
5. Serve with your favorite toppings, or try the **ALMOND BUTTER SYRUP (PAGE 34)**.

D **gL** **gR** **pL** **vE** **vT**

MAKES 4 WAFFLES

**PER SERVING
(1 WAFFLE)**

Calories: 272

Calories from Fat: 298

Total Fat: 5g, 8%

Saturated Fat: 4g, 20%

Total Carb: 50g, 17%

Dietary Fiber: 2g, 8%

Sugars: 8g

Protein: 7g

Cholesterol: 3mg, 1%

Sodium: 498mg, 21%

Belgian Sweet Waffles

Belgian Liège waffles elevate traditional waffles to a whole new level of delicious. Made with a rich, yeast-based dough, they are cooked with giant crystals of sugar and taste as good for dessert as they do for breakfast. Because of the natural density that almond flour lends to baked goods, it's easy to create Liège-inspired waffles without the yeast and without all the extra prep work the classic Belgian version requires. This version bakes up soft and sweet and tastes good slathered in syrup, topped with fresh fruit, or dolloped with whipped cream, but can stand alone as a truly delicious breakfast all on its own. Instead of pearl sugar, this recipe calls for Sucanat, which is a coarse natural sugar. Feel free to skip the sugar if you prefer.

4 eggs

1 cup almond flour

¼ teaspoon salt

1 teaspoon baking powder

1 tablespoon pure vanilla extract

2 tablespoons honey or agave nectar

4 teaspoons Sucanat (optional)

1. Preheat a waffle iron.
2. In a large bowl, whisk together the eggs, almond flour, salt, baking powder, vanilla, and honey until a smooth batter forms.
3. Spray the waffle iron with nonstick cooking spray, then, for each waffle, spoon the batter on, sprinkle with 1 teaspoon of Sucanat and cook it according to manufacturer's instructions until it's golden brown. Remove from the oven and serve as desired.

gL
gR
nL
VT

MAKES 4 WAFFLES

**PER SERVING
(1 WAFFLE)**

Calories: 236

Calories from Fat: 71

Total Fat: 4g, 6%

Saturated Fat: 1g, 5%

Total Carb: 38g, 13%

Dietary Fiber: 1g, 4%

Sugars: 14g

Protein: 9g

Cholesterol: 164mg, 55%

Sodium: 360mg, 15%

Top Your Waffles!

Here are a few favorite waffle toppers that can turn those morning blues into morning yahoos!

Very Berry. Fresh or frozen blueberries, strawberries, raspberries, or boysenberries, heated with a tablespoon of honey or pure maple syrup.

Bananarama. Sliced bananas pair perfectly with waffles. Add fresh whipped cream and a drizzle of pure maple syrup to really finish your breakfast off in style.

Choco Yum Yum. Like chocolate chip cookies? Slather almond butter atop your waffles, sprinkle with chocolate chips, and drizzle with pure maple syrup. It tastes just like a cookie!

Sweet and Savory. Top your waffle with slices of bacon and a poached egg for a rich, delicious breakfast dish.

Custardy French Toast with Raspberry Almond Butter Syrup

French toast is usually made with an egg, but this vegan version uses everything almond to make an unbelievably delicious, custard-inspired French toast that will melt in your mouth. Topped with a homemade raspberry almond syrup, the flavors of this breakfast are warm, rich, and inviting. Perfect for lazy weekend mornings, brunches, and those nights when you want to eat breakfast for dinner.

gL
vE
vT

MAKES 8 SERVINGS

FOR THE FRENCH TOAST

1 cup almond milk

½ cup almond butter

⅓ cup almond flour

3 tablespoons coconut oil or Earth Balance, melted

1 tablespoon pure vanilla extract

8 large, thick slices of day-old bread (gluten-free, if desired)

FOR THE SYRUP

⅔ cup pure maple syrup

2 tablespoons almond extract

1 pint fresh raspberries

**PER SERVING
(1 TOAST)**

Calories: 327

Calories from Fat: 190

Total Fat: 15g, 23%

Saturated Fat: 6g, 30%

Total Carb: 41g, 14%

Dietary Fiber: 7g, 28%

Sugars: 19g

Protein: 7g

Cholesterol: 2mg, 1%

Sodium: 153mg, 6%

1. In a blender, mix together the almond milk, almond butter, almond flour, coconut oil, and vanilla until smooth. Pour into a shallow dish.
2. Spray a griddle with nonstick cooking spray or coat it with a small amount of melted coconut oil.
3. Dip the slices of bread into the almond custard coating. Transfer them to the hot griddle and cook until golden brown, about 2–3 minutes. Flip the bread and cook on the other side until golden brown, another 2–3 minutes. Serve immediately.
4. To make the syrup, combine the maple syrup with the almond extract in a saucepan over medium heat. Heat until very warm, then remove it from heat and toss in the raspberries. Serve in heaping spoonfuls over the hot slices of French toast.

Banana Bread Oatmeal

This piping-hot bowl of oats will send you to oatmeal heaven. It tastes like a bowl of banana bread and is a great way to use ripe bananas. Not so fond of hot cereal? Give this a try. With the creamy sweetness of mashed banana and the tart goodness of fresh blueberries, you might become a convert.

D
GL
VE
VT

½ cup quick oats (gluten-free if desired)

1 ripe banana, mashed

1 cup almond milk

4 tablespoons almond butter

2 tablespoons maple syrup

½ teaspoon cinnamon

1 cup fresh blueberries

1. In a medium saucepan, combine the oats, banana, almond milk, and almond butter. Cook over medium heat for 3–5 minutes, or until the preferred thickness is reached.

2. Remove the oatmeal from the heat and spoon it into bowls. Drizzle it with the maple syrup, sprinkle it with the cinnamon, and serve it topped with the blueberries.

MAKES 2 SERVINGS

PER SERVING (½ RECIPE)

Calories: 663

Calories from Fat: 436

Total Fat: 23g, 35%

Saturated Fat: 4g, 20%

Total Carb: 98g, 33%

Dietary Fiber: 14g, 56%

Sugars: 31g

Protein: 22g

Cholesterol: 9mg, 3%

Sodium: 348mg, 14%

Overnight Almond Butter Oats with Fresh Peaches and Cream

Cooking oatmeal overnight is the easiest way to have breakfast waiting and ready to go the minute you awake. Convenience is one thing—but this is also outstandingly delicious. If you're looking for a vegan way to serve this recipe, swap the cream for soy-based cream. No other substitutions are needed. This recipe is absolute perfection right from the crockpot.

D
gL
VE
VT

FOR THE MAPLED OATS

4 cups water

2 cups vanilla almond milk

2 cups Coach's Steel Cut Oats (or certified gluten-free oats)

¼ cup pure maple syrup, honey, or brown sugar

½ cup almond butter

1 teaspoon cinnamon

¾ teaspoon salt

FOR THE PEACHES AND CREAM

2 fresh peaches, skinned and sliced thin

1 cup cream or nondairy almond milk coffee creamer

1. Spray the inside of a 4–5 quart slow cooker generously with nonstick cooking spray.
2. In the crockpot, stir together the water, almond milk, oats, maple syrup, almond butter cinnamon, and salt. Cover and cook it on low overnight, for up to 8 hours.
3. In the morning, spoon the oatmeal into bowls, top with the fresh peach slices and pour a small amount of coffee creamer over the oatmeal. Serve immediately.

Note: This recipe calls for steel-cut oats and has been written using directions that work with Coach's Oats, since that brand is easily available nationwide.

MAKES 8 SERVINGS

**PER SERVING
(⅛ RECIPE)**

Calories: 401

Calories from Fat: 79

Total Fat: 22g, 34%

Saturated Fat: 8g, 40%

Total Carb: 41g, 14%

Dietary Fiber: 6g, 24%

Sugars: 11g

Protein: 13g

Cholesterol: 43mg, 14%

Sodium: 314mg, 13%

McMuffin Morning Munchers

Wake up to a combination of sweet and salty with this delicious morning muffin mix. The combination of almond butter, bacon, and banana is so good, it's inspired. A quick, simple recipe to whip up on busy mornings.

2 English muffins (gluten-free if preferred), toasted

4 tablespoons almond butter

4 slices bacon or vegan bacon, cooked

1 banana, sliced thin

2 tablespoons pure maple syrup

1. Spread the almond butter on the toasted English muffins. Place the bacon and banana slices on top. Drizzle with the maple syrup and serve.

MAKES 2 SERVINGS

PER SERVING (1 MUFFIN)

Calories: 690

Calories from Fat: 316

Total Fat: 36g, 55%

Saturated Fat: 8g, 40%

Total Carb: 66g, 22%

Dietary Fiber: 7g, 28%

Sugars: 17g

Protein: 28g

Cholesterol: 55mg, 18%

Sodium: 1526 mg, 64%

Almond Butter Breakfast Sandwiches

If you're looking for a quick, hearty breakfast that is also full of flavor, this easy sandwich is just the recipe for you. Seed-speckled bread is topped with a schmear of almond butter, then served with bacon and thinly sliced apple. Of course, if you're not concerned about eating a gluten-free diet, feel free to substitute any of your favorite slices of bread. Just keep in mind that the crunchier, heartier breads taste the best.

2 tablespoons almond butter

2 slices gluten-free sunflower seed bread, toasted

2 slices turkey bacon or vegan bacon, cooked until crispy

½ green apple, thinly sliced

Sea salt

1. Spread the almond butter on the toasted bread. Top with bacon and apple slices. Sprinkle lightly with salt. Place the second piece of toast on top of the sandwich and slice in half. Serve immediately.

GL VE VT

MAKES 1 SANDWICH

**PER SERVING
(1 SANDWICH)**

Calories: 674

Calories from Fat: 374

Total Fat: 41.6g, 64%

Saturated Fat: 3.4g, 17%

Trans Fat: 0.0g

Cholesterol: 30mg, 10%

Total Carb: 59.9g, 20%

Dietary Fiber: 14.5g, 58%

Sugars: 511.4g

Protein: 28,6g

Cholesterol: 41mg

Sodium: 541mg, 23%

Almond Toast a Go-Go

A piece of toast with sliced avocado is about as easy as breakfast foods get. This simple twist on classic avocado toast lends a little more flavor and a lot more protein to your mornings. The creaminess of ripe avocado tastes incredible when paired with the nutty goodness of almond butter. Creamy or crunchy almond butters both work well in this recipe.

2 tablespoons roasted almond butter

2 pieces of sourdough bread (gluten-free, if desired), toasted

1 slice sharp cheddar cheese or vegan cheddar

2 slices bacon or vegan bacon, halved

1 avocado, sliced

1. Spread the almond butter on the toast. Top each piece of toast with a slice of cheddar, two slices of bacon, and slices of avocado. Serve immediately.

GF
VE
VT

MAKES 2 SERVINGS

**PER SERVING
(1 TOAST)**

Calories: 602

Calories from Fat: 346

Total Fat: 38.4g, 59%

Saturated Fat: Fat
   8.2g, 41%

Trans Fat: 0.0g

Total Carb: 39.8g,
   13%

Dietary Fiber: 10.3g,
   41%

Sugars: 3.4g

Protein: 21.4g

Cholesterol: 30mg,
   10%

Sodium: 730mg, 30%

Vanilla-Almond Crunch Granola

Inspired by a favorite recipe from fellow blogger Sophistimom, this simple gra-nola is easy to make, and even easier to eat until it's all gone. The hearty good-ness of flax and oats comes together with the natural sweetness of honey. A sprinkling of almond flour lends texture and a mild nuttiness to the final product, making a homemade granola that is better than any you can buy in the store.

D
gL
gR
VE
VT

6 cups old-fashioned oats

½ cup sliced almonds

⅔ cup almond flour

½ cup flaxseeds

½ cup coconut oil

1 ½ cups honey

1 tablespoon pure vanilla extract

½ teaspoon pure almond extract

1. Preheat the oven to 300°F.
2. Line a large baking sheet with parchment paper.
3. In a large bowl, stir together the oats, almonds, almond flour, and flaxseeds. Add the coconut oil, honey, vanilla, and almond extract and stir all the ingredients until well combined.
4. Turn the granola onto the lined baking sheet. Bake in the preheated oven for 15 minutes, then use a spatula to turn the mixture and continue baking for another 15 minutes, or until the oats are light golden brown.
5. Cool it completely, then break the granola into small pieces. Store in an airtight container for up to 7 days.

MAKES 12 SERVINGS

PER SERVING (¹⁄₁₂ RECIPE)

Calories: 263

Calories from Fat: 117

Total Fat: 13.0g, 20%

Saturated Fat: 8.2g, 41%

Trans Fat: 0.0g

Total Carb: 35.9g, 12%

Dietary Fiber: 3.1g, 12%

Sugars: 35.1g

Protein: 2.8g

Cholesterol: 0mg, 0%

Sodium: 4mg, 0%

Cavegirl Granola

Granola made without grains. That's the idea behind this delicious almond, almond, almond granola, which bakes up crunchy and just sweet enough to feel like a treat. Serve in a bowl with almond milk and berries for a truly scrumptious bowl of breakfast.

1 cup sliced almonds
½ cup pumpkin seeds
½ cup almond flour
¾ cup unsweetened shredded coconut
1 tablespoon pumpkin pie spice
3 tablespoons coconut oil, melted
3 tablespoons honey or pure maple syrup
1 tablespoon pure vanilla extract

1. Preheat the oven to 325°F.
2. In a large bowl, stir together the almonds, pumpkin seeds, almond flour, coconut, and pumpkin pie spice.
3. In a small bowl, whisk together the coconut oil, honey, and vanilla. Pour over the dry ingredients and stir it until well coated.
4. Spread the granola on a parchment-lined baking sheet. Bake for 40–50 minutes, stirring the granola mixture every 10 minutes.
5. Once the mixture is golden brown, remove it from the oven and allow it to cool completely. As it cools, the granola will begin to crisp. Store it in an airtight container for up to 1 week.

D **gL** **gR** **nL** **VE** **VT**

MAKES 10 SERVINGS

PER SERVING
(¹⁄₁₀ **RECIPE**)
Calories: 173
Calories from Fat: 126
Total Fat: 14.0g, 22%
Saturated Fat: 6.3g, 32%
Total Carb: 9.9g, 3%
Dietary Fiber: 2.1g, 8%
Sugars: 6.2g
Protein: 4.0g
Cholesterol: 0mg, 0%
Sodium: 3mg, 0%

Crispy Granola Bars

Bake these quick and hearty granola bars on the weekend and have a nutritious grab-and-go snack available all week long. If you're not watching your sugar intake, corn syrup works as an excellent binder for these bars, but agave nectar will work, too.

D
GL
VE
VT

½ cup agave nectar or corn syrup

¼ cup brown sugar

¼ cup coconut oil, butter, or Earth Balance, melted

½ cup creamy almond butter

1 teaspoon pure vanilla extract

½ teaspoon cinnamon

2 cups quick-cooking oats (gluten-free, if desired)

2 cups brown rice crispy cereal

½ cup golden raisins

¼ cup dried cranberries

¼ cup chopped almonds or walnuts

1. In a large, microwave-safe bowl, melt the agave nectar, brown sugar, coconut oil, almond butter, vanilla, and cinnamon together in the microwave for 90 seconds.
2. Stir the mixture, then microwave it for another 60 seconds.
3. Add the oats, cereal, raisins, cranberries, and almonds to the mixture. Stir to coat.
4. Pour the mixture into an 8 × 8-inch baking dish lined with parchment or sprayed with nonstick cooking spray. Press the mixture down firmly with your fingers to pack the bars.
5. Refrigerate it for an hour before slicing into 10 bars. Serve them immediately or wrap in plastic wrap and store in the fridge for up to 1 week.

MAKES 10 SERVINGS

PER SERVING (1 BAR)

Calories: 301

Calories from Fat: 135

Total Fat: 15.0g, 23%

Saturated Fat: 5.5g, 27%

Trans Fat: 0.0g

Total Carb: 40.2g, 13%

Dietary Fiber: 3.8g, 15%

Sugars: 13.0g

Protein: 6.3g

Cholesterol: 0mg, 0%

Sodium: 49mg, 2%

Cranberry Breakfast Bars

These delicious bars are perfect for those busy mornings when you need a grab-and-go breakfast. They're easy to make ahead by stirring the ingredients together and baking the bars during dinner. Allow them to cool overnight, and you'll wake up to a ready-to-go breakfast the moment the sun rises.

¼ cup avocado or coconut oil

5 tablespoons raw honey or agave nectar

1 ½ cups almond flour

½ cup unsweetened shredded coconut

½ teaspoon baking powder

½ teaspoon sea salt

¼ cup pistachios or macadamia nuts, chopped

½ cup dried cranberries or dried cherries

1. Preheat the oven to 350°F.
2. In a large bowl, whisk together the oil (if using coconut oil, melt it in a microwave-safe bowl before whisking) and honey.
3. Add the almond flour, coconut, baking powder, salt, pistachios, and cranberries to the bowl. Stir until the mixture is well combined.
4. Press the mixture into an 8 × 8-inch baking dish lined with parchment paper.
5. Bake for 18–22 minutes, or just until the edges of the mixture turn light golden brown. Remove from the oven and cool completely before slicing it into bars.

D gL gR pL vE vT

MAKES 12 BARS

PER SERVING (1 BAR)

Calories: 166

Calories from Fat: 16

Total Fat: 7g, 11%

Saturated Fat: 2g, 10%

Total Carb: 26g, 9%

Dietary Fiber: 3g, 12%

Sugars: 11g

Protein: 2g, 5%

Cholesterol: 0mg, 0%

Sodium: 120mg, 5%

No-Bake Almond Butter Bites

Many commercial protein bars are packed with unnecessary ingredients and fillers. Here's a healthier and less expensive option. These easy no-bake almond butter bites are just sweet enough to taste like a treat, but are packed with healthy, whole ingredients that will keep you fueled for a good long while.

1 ¾ cups old-fashioned oats (gluten-free if desired)

¼ cup dried cherries, diced

¼ cup dark chocolate chips

½ cup maple syrup (Grade B if possible)

½ cup almond butter

1. Combine all of the ingredients in a bowl and stir well to combine.
2. Press the oat mixture into an 8 × 8-inch pan and refrigerate for 1½ hours.
3. Cut the mixture into 8 pieces. Store them in the refrigerator or freezer for up to 1 week.

GF VE VT

MAKES 8 BARS

**PER SERVING
(1 BAR)**

Calories: 234

Calories from Fat: 101

Total Fat: 11.2g, 17%

Saturated Fat: 1.7g, 8%

Total Carb: 30.3g, 10%

Dietary Fiber: 2.3g, 9%

Sugars: 14.2g

Protein: 5.8g

Cholesterol: 0mg, 0%

Sodium: 2mg, 0%

Thai-Style Breakfast Burritos

Looking for a fun way to spice up your mornings? Try this quick and simple recipe for breakfast burritos with a Thai twist. The secret to this scrumptious morning wrap is the almond butter and green curry sauce. If you're new to green curry paste, you can find it in the Asian section of most grocery stores. It's a mild, slightly spicy sauce that lends mouth-popping flavor to any meal, especially this one. Need more protein? This recipe pairs well with a handful of chopped rotisserie chicken.

1 tablespoon green curry paste

3 tablespoons almond butter

2 flour tortillas or gluten-free tortillas, warmed

4 eggs, scrambled

½ cup Monterey Jack cheese, shredded

1 red bell pepper, thinly sliced

½ cup fresh cilantro

2 tablespoons Sriracha

1. In a small bowl, mix together the green curry paste and almond butter.
2. Spread half of this sauce into the center of each tortilla.
3. Top with the hot scrambled eggs and cheese.
4. Layer the fresh red pepper slices and a bunch of fresh cilantro on top of the cheese.
5. Roll up the tortillas and serve with Sriracha.

MAKES 2 BURRITOS

**PER SERVING
(1 BURRITO)**

Calories: 559

Calories from Fat: 297

Total Fat: 35g 54%

Saturated Fat: 11g
   55%

Total Carb: 35g 12%

Dietary Fiber: 7g 28%

Sugars: 4g

Protein: 29g

Cholesterol: 357mg
   119%

Sodium: 647mg 27%

4

Breads and Muffins

In the age of gluten-free, low-carb, zero-allergen, no-animal eating, almond products make it easy to enjoy some of your favorite foods from childhood without feeling like you have to go without. Skipping out on white bread, peanut butter, and creamy dairy products isn't difficult when you have rich, flavorful almond products to replace the less-healthful ingredients like refined white flour and sugar.

When it comes to breads, how do you hit the kitchen and start cooking without making a mess with substitutions and ingredient swaps for flour, baking powder, and eggs? This chapter takes the guesswork out of breads and quick breads. With a focus on recipes for the gluten-free, vegan, and paleo eater, the majority of recipes in this section are made with only almond flour (rather than white flour) and offer tasty, almond-based alternatives for breads you already love. Grab a bowl and start baking! You're about to discover a dozen new ways to cook your favorite baked treats in a more healthful way.

MUFFIN MIX-INS

The **PALEO ALMOND FLOUR MUFFINS** and **VEGAN ALMOND FLOUR MUFFINS** on **PAGES 54** and **55** are great for breakfast. They're sweet, soft, vanilla-flavored pastries, perfect all by themselves. But, I daresay they're even better when they become your muffin favorites! Stir up a batch of these basic muffins, then turn them into any of these flavors by mixing a few ingredients into the batter. The variations are endless, but here are a few favorites.

» **Apple Streusel.** Stir 1 peeled, diced apple and ½ tablespoon of cinnamon into the batter. Top with **ALMOND FLOUR STREUSEL TOPPING (PAGE 56)**.

» **Blueberry.** Stir 1 cup fresh or frozen blueberries into the batter before baking.

» **Cranberry-Lemon.** Stir 1 cup fresh or frozen cranberries and the zest of one lemon into the batter. Add lemon zest and ¼ teaspoon nutmeg to the **ALMOND FLOUR STREUSEL TOPPING (PAGE 56)** and sprinkle it atop the batter before baking the muffins.

» **Chocolate Espresso.** Replace ¼ cup of almond flour with unsweetened cocoa powder. Add 1 teaspoon instant coffee and 1 cup dark chocolate chips to the batter.

» **Almond Poppy Seed.** Add 1 teaspoon almond extract and 1 tablespoon of poppy seeds to the batter. Add the zest of 1 lemon to the **ALMOND FLOUR STREUSEL TOPPING (PAGE 56)**, and sprinkle it atop the batter before baking.

» **Chocolate Chip.** Stir 1 cup dark chocolate chips into your muffin batter before baking.

Mile-High Biscuits

This recipe works best with very finely ground blanched almond flour. The biscuits bake up full and soft and are best when served straight out of the oven, whether for breakfast, brunch, or dinner. Slather with honey butter or gravy for a truly delicious side.

2 ½ cups blanched almond flour + 2 tablespoons for dusting

½ teaspoon salt

¾ teaspoon baking soda

¼ cup butter or Earth Balance

2 eggs

1 tablespoon raw honey or agave nectar

1. Preheat the oven to 350°F.
2. Line a baking sheet with parchment paper.
3. In a large bowl, stir together the almond flour, salt, and baking soda. Mix in the butter, using a fork.
4. Stir in the eggs and honey until dough forms.
5. Place the dough on a wooden cutting board dusted with almond flour and roll out until 1 ½ inches thick.
6. Use a knife to cut the biscuits into 9 squares.
7. Transfer the biscuits to the lined baking sheet. Bake for 12–15 minutes, or until the biscuits are golden brown.

MAKES 9 BISCUITS

**PER SERVING
(1 BISCUIT)**

Calories: 75

Calories from Fat: 55

Total Fat: 7g, 11%

Saturated Fat: 4g, 20%

Total Carb: 2g, 1%

Dietary Fiber: 0g, 0%

Sugars: 2g

Protein: 1g

Cholesterol: 53mg, 18%

Sodium: 234mg, 10%

Paleo Almond Flour Muffins

These easy almond flour muffins are perfect for paleo eaters. They are simple and nicely sweetened, the perfect muffin to add variations to. I've included a box of mix-in ideas on page 52 to easily turn this muffin into a bakery-style treat.

(gL)
(gR)
(pL)
(vT)

¼ cup honey

¼ cup avocado oil (grapeseed oil is okay if you're not following a paleo eating plan)

¼ cup almond milk

2 eggs

1 teaspoon pure vanilla extract

2 ½ cups blanched almond flour

¾ teaspoon baking powder

½ teaspoon salt

Special Equipment: Muffin tin or popover pan; cupcake liners

1. Preheat the oven to 350°F.
2. In a large bowl, whisk together the honey, oil, almond milk, eggs, and vanilla.
3. Add the almond flour, baking powder, and salt to the mixture. Stir until the batter becomes smooth.
4. Spoon the batter into a muffin tin lined with cupcake liners.
5. Bake for 16–20 minutes, or just until the muffins are light, golden brown and bounce back when touched lightly in the center.
6. Remove from the oven and cool before serving.

MAKES 12 MUFFINS

**PER SERVING
(1 MUFFIN)**

Calories: 205

Calories from Fat: 12

Total Fat: 2g, 3%

Saturated Fat: 0g, 0%

Total Carb: 44g, 15%

Dietary Fiber: 1g, 4%

Sugars: 24g

Protein: 4g

Cholesterol: 28mg, 9%

Sodium: 145mg, 6%

Vegan Almond Flour Muffins

You can serve this mildly sweet muffin on its own or mix in a variety of ingredients to create your favorite morning flavors. Check the box insert on page 52 for a few of my favorite ideas.

2 tablespoons flaxseed meal

½ cup warm water

2 tablespoons coconut oil, melted

1 tablespoon pure vanilla extract

⅓ cup agave nectar or pure maple syrup

¾ cup almond milk

2 cups blanched almond flour

2 ½ teaspoons baking powder

½ teaspoon salt

Special Equipment: Muffin tin or popover pan; cupcake liners

1. Preheat the oven to 350°F.
2. In a large bowl, whisk together the flaxseed meal and warm water. Allow to sit until thickened, about 2 to 3 minutes.
3. Add the coconut oil, vanilla, maple syrup, and almond milk. Whisk together until well combined.
4. Add the almond flour, baking powder, and salt. Stir together until a smooth batter forms.
5. Spoon the batter into a muffin tin lined with cupcake liners.
6. Bake for 18–21 minutes, or until golden brown.

(D) (gL) (gR) (DL) (VE) (VT)

MAKES 12 MUFFINS

PER SERVING (1 MUFFIN)

Calories: 199

Calories from Fat: 136

Total Fat: 15.1g, 23%

Saturated Fat: 5.8g, 29%

Total Carb: 11.3g, 4%

Dietary Fiber: 2.8g, 11%

Sugars: 5.8g

Protein: 4.7g

Cholesterol: 0mg, 0%

Sodium: 108mg, 5%

Almond Flour Streusel Topping

Mix up a batch of this simple almond flour streusel topping and sprinkle it on your muffins for bakery-style flair. If you're avoiding refined sugar, you can stir in ½ tablespoon of honey or agave nectar, but the streusel won't bake up as crunchy as it does with the grainy Sucanat.

½ cup almond flour

1 ½ tablespoons coconut oil, butter, or Earth Balance

2 tablespoons Sucanat

¼ teaspoon cinnamon (optional)

1. Use a fork to mix all the ingredients together until coarse and crumbly.
2. Sprinkle it over muffins before baking, or on top of pancakes, oatmeal, or your favorite frosted cupcakes.

D **gL** **gR** **pL** **VE** **VT**

MAKES 12 TABLESPOONS

PER SERVING (1 TABLESPOON)

Calories: 65

Calories from Fat: 54

Total Fat: 6.0g, 9%

Saturated Fat: 2.5g, 13%

Trans Fat: 0.0g

Total Carb: 1.6g, 1%

Dietary Fiber: 0.8g, 3%

Protein: 1.5g

Cholesterol: 0mg, 0%

Sodium: 3mg, 0%

Zucchini Muffins

Zucchini with a touch of almond butter is a delicious combination of flavor and texture. These sweet muffins make gorgeous early-morning eats and pair perfectly with an ice-cold glass of almond milk. This recipe calls for coconut flour, which has become a popular baking alternative for many paleo and gluten-free eaters because of its high nutrient and protein content. This recipe is a good way to familiarize yourself with the texture and flavor of coconut flour. If you can't find it, feel free to swap an equivalent amount of white flour or gluten-free flour into this recipe instead.

4 eggs

2 tablespoons butter or coconut oil, melted

⅓ cup honey or agave nectar

1 teaspoon pure vanilla extract

½ cup coconut flour

½ cup blanched almond flour

1 tablespoon cinnamon

1 teaspoon baking powder

1 ½ cups zucchini, grated (about 3 small zucchini)

Special Equipment: Muffin tin or popover pan; cupcake liners

1. Preheat the oven to 350°F.
2. In a large bowl or stand mixer, beat together the eggs, butter, honey, and vanilla until well mixed.
3. Add the coconut flour, almond flour, cinnamon, and baking powder. Mix until smooth.
4. Fold in the zucchini.
5. Spoon the batter into a muffin tin lined with cupcake liners.
6. Bake for 18–22 minutes, or until the center of the muffins spring back when touched lightly.

D **gL** **gR** **pL** **vT**

MAKES 8 MUFFINS

PER SERVING (1 MUFFIN)

Calories: 181

Calories from Fat: 83

Total Fat: 9.2g, 14%

Saturated Fat: 3.0g, 15%

Trans Fat: 0.0g

Total Carb: 19.1g, 6%

Dietary Fiber: 4.0g, 16%

Sugars: 12.7g

Protein: 5g

Cholesterol: 89mg, 30%

Sodium: 72mg, 3%

Pumpkin-Almond Donut Muffins

Donuts you don't have to feel guilty over? Believe it! Toss the traditional white flour and use almond flour instead. These fun, baked treats cook like a muffin but taste like a donut. Be sure to use very finely ground blanched almond flour for best results.

Ⓓ
ⓖ ᴸ
ⓖ ᴿ
ⓥ ᵀ

FOR THE DONUTS

2 ½ cups blanched almond flour

1 teaspoon baking soda

½ teaspoon kosher salt

1 ½ teaspoons pumpkin pie spice

2 large eggs

½ cup raw honey, agave nectar, or maple syrup

½ cup pumpkin puree

¼ cup olive oil

FOR THE GLAZE

¼ cup melted butter or coconut oil

⅔ cup light brown sugar or Sucanat

1 teaspoon cinnamon

Special Equipment: Muffin tin or popover pan; cupcake liners

1. Preheat the oven to 350°F.
2. In a large bowl, combine the almond flour, baking soda, salt, and pumpkin pie spice. Stir well.
3. Whisk the eggs in a medium bowl. Add the honey, pumpkin puree, and olive oil. Whisk until smooth. Pour the egg mixture into the flour mixture and stir well to combine.
4. Pour 1 tablespoon of the batter into each of approximately 30 muffin cups lined with cupcake liners. (You may have a little more or a little less.) Bake for 15 minutes, or until brown. Insert a toothpick into a muffin. If it comes out clean, they're done.

MAKES APPROXIMATELY 30 MUFFINS

PER SERVING (1 MUFFIN)

Calories: 117

Calories from Fat: 72

Total Fat: 3g, 5%

Saturated Fat: 2g, 10%

Total Carb: 18g, 6%

Dietary Fiber: 0g, 0%

Sugars: 10g

Protein: 2g

Cholesterol: 12mg, 4%

Sodium: 59mg, 2%

5. Let the muffins cool until they can be handled. To prepare the glaze, place the melted butter in one small, shallow dish and stir the sugar and cinnamon together in a second dish. Dip the muffin tops in butter, then roll them in the cinnamon-sugar mixture to coat. Let the muffins rest on wire racks. Store them in an airtight container for up to 3 days.

Sweet Corn Muffins

Craving cornbread? These easy corn muffins are the perfect side to serve with chili, beef stew, and Mexican dishes. They're light, soft, and tasty. Better yet, they make a great base for all sorts of delicious mix-ins. Check out the opposite page for a few favorites.

2 tablespoons flaxseed meal

½ cup warm water

1 ⅓ cups cornmeal

1 ⅓ cups blanched almond flour

4 tablespoons Earth Balance, melted

1 ½ teaspoons baking powder

½ teaspoon salt

½ cup almond milk

4 tablespoons honey

Special Equipment: Muffin tin or popover pan; cupcake liners

1. Preheat the oven to 350°F.
2. In a large bowl, whisk together the flaxseed meal and water. Allow to set until thickened.
3. Add the cornmeal, almond flour, Earth Balance, baking powder, salt, almond milk, and honey. Stir together until smooth.
4. Spoon the batter into a muffin tin lined with cupcake liners.
5. Bake for 16 to 20 minutes, or until the center of the muffins springs back when touched lightly.

D **gL** **gR** **vE** **vT**

MAKES 12 MUFFINS

PER SERVING (1 MUFFIN)

Calories: 207

Calories from Fat: 117

Total Fat: 13.0g, 20%

Saturated Fat: 5.1g, 25%

Total Carb: 19.4g, 6%

Dietary Fiber: 3.0g, 12%

Sugars: 6.2g

Protein: 4.4g

Cholesterol: 10mg, 3%

Sodium: 233mg, 10%

Corn Muffin Mix-Ins

These muffins are so easy to upgrade! Stir in these ingredient combos and turn your basic muffins into gourmet-inspired sides.

Classic Corn. ½ cup frozen corn

Jalapeño-Cheddar. 1 chopped jalapeño and ½ cup sharp cheddar or vegan cheddar

Bacon-Onion. ¼ cup bacon bits or vegan bacon bits and 2 tablespoons chopped scallions

Mexi Confetti. 2 tablespoons chopped red bell pepper, 2 tablespoons chopped purple onion, 2 tablespoons frozen corn, and 2 tablespoons chopped green chile

Almond Butter Muffins

These muffins bake up light brown, soft, and full of delicious banana-almond flavor. The big surprise? They're made without any flour at all! Perfect for make-ahead breakfasts, they also pack nicely in school lunches and snack packs. Try serving them warm with a slather of butter and jam, or eat them as they are. These muffins are good enough to go au naturel but make for a fun canvas for those ingredients you already love slathering in the middle of your muffins.

D
gL
gR
pL
VE
VT

3 very ripe bananas

1 ¼ cups almond butter

¼ cup honey or agave nectar

3 eggs

1 tablespoon pure vanilla extract

1 teaspoon baking powder

½ teaspoon cinnamon

½ cup dark chocolate chips (optional)

Special Equipment: Muffin tin or popover pan; cupcake liners

1. Preheat the oven to 350°F.
2. In a large bowl or stand mixer, beat together the bananas and almond butter until smooth.
3. Add the honey, eggs, vanilla, baking powder, and cinnamon and beat until well mixed into the batter. Stir in the chocolate chips (if desired).
4. Spoon the batter into the muffin tin lined with cupcake liners.
5. Bake for 18–21 minutes, or just until the center of the muffins spring back when touched lightly.

MAKES 12 MUFFINS

**PER SERVING
(1 MUFFIN)**

Calories: 256

Calories from Fat: 155

Total Fat: 17.2g, 26%

Saturated Fat: 2.6g, 13%

Trans Fat: 0.0g

Total Carb: 21.0g 7%

Dietary Fiber: 1.8g 7%

Sugars: 12.3g

Protein: 7.6g

Cholesterol: 41mg, 14%

Sodium: 16mg, 1%

Cheddar Dill Popovers

The mellow bite of cheddar combined with the zesty addition of dill makes these savory popovers delicious for breakfast, brunch, or as a dinner side dish.

1 tablespoon unsalted butter or Earth Balance

1 cup unsweetened almond milk

2 eggs

1 cup flour

½ cup extra-sharp cheddar

½ teaspoon kosher salt

Freshly ground black pepper

2 tablespoons fresh dill

Special Equipment: Popover pan or muffin tin

1. Preheat the oven to 400°F.
2. Melt the butter in a small microwavable bowl for 20 seconds on high.
3. Microwave the almond milk in a large microwavable bowl for 1 minute on high.
4. Brush the inside and tops of a popover pan with the butter. Place the pan in the oven.
5. Working quickly, place the almond milk, eggs, and flour in a large bowl and whisk to combine.
6. Add the cheddar, salt, pepper, and dill and whisk well.
7. Remove the hot pan from the oven and fill the cups ¾ full with the popover batter. Place the tin in the oven and bake for 35–40 minutes. (Don't open the oven door for the first 35 minutes of baking because that will cause the popovers to collapse. Check them after 35 minutes to make sure they're done, because they will be solid by then.)
8. If the popovers aren't quite done, bake for 5–8 minutes more. Serve immediately.

MAKES 6 POPOVERS

PER SERVING (1 POPOVER)

Calories: 98

Calories from Fat: 73

Total Fat: 8g, 12%

Saturated Fat: 5g, 25%

Total Carb: 19g, 6%

Dietary Fiber: 1g, 4%

Sugars: 2g

Protein: 8g

Cholesterol: 74mg, 25%

Sodium: 306mg, 13%

Cherry Almond Scones

Raw almond butter adds a mild sweetness and a pop of flavor to these classic scones. Combining the tartness of dried cherries and a sprinkling of cinnamon, these beauties are perfect for breakfast or afternoon tea. Swap in a gluten-free flour mix to enjoy them on a g-free diet.

MAKES 8 SCONES

PER SERVING (1 SCONE)

Calories: 259
Calories from Fat: 95
Total Fat: 1g, 2%
Saturated Fat: 0g, 0%
Total Carb: 25g, 8%
Dietary Fiber: 2g, 8%
Sugars: 6g
Protein: 1g
Cholesterol: 0mg, 0%
Sodium: 337mg, 14%

5 tablespoons unsalted butter
2 ¼ cups unbleached all-purpose flour or **ALL-PURPOSE GLUTEN-FREE ALMOND FLOUR MIX (PAGE 27)**
1 tablespoon baking powder
4 tablespoons sugar
½ teaspoon salt
1 cup dried cherries
1 cup + 1 tablespoon unsweetened almond milk
1 tablespoon raw almond butter
½ teaspoon cinnamon

1. Preheat the oven to 425°F. Place butter in the freezer for 10 minutes.
2. Place 2 cups of the flour and the baking powder, sugar, and salt in a food processor fitted with a metal blade. Pulse to mix.
3. Quickly grate the butter on a cheese grater over the bowl of the food processor and add the cherries. Pulse a few times to mix. Scrape the dough into a large bowl and fold in 1 cup of the almond milk, the almond butter, and the cinnamon until combined well.
4. Sprinkle the remaining ¼ cup flour on a work surface and knead the dough quickly until it just comes together. (Do not overknead.) Pat out the dough to a 1-inch thickness. Using a pastry cutter or sharp knife, cut the dough into eight triangles.
5. Transfer the dough to a cookie sheet and brush with the remaining 1 tablespoon of almond milk. Bake for 18–25 minutes, or until the scones are golden brown. Insert a toothpick into the center. If it comes out clean, the scones are done.

Banana Almond Bread

Classic banana bread gets an almond twist with this dense, moist, flavor-packed loaf. This recipe is easy to follow, foolproof, and each slice packs more than 11 grams of protein! It's a snack that satiates your hunger while feeding your cravings for truly good food.

3 cups almond flour

1 ½ teaspoons baking powder

1 ½ teaspoons cinnamon

¼ teaspoon allspice

½ teaspoon kosher salt

2 very ripe large bananas

3 large eggs

¼ cup maple syrup or raw honey

¼ cup unsalted butter or coconut oil

1. Preheat the oven to 350°F. Grease a 9 × 5 bread loaf pan.
2. In a large bowl, mix together the flour, baking powder, cinnamon, allspice, and salt.
3. In a separate bowl, mash the bananas with a fork or potato masher. Stir in the eggs, maple syrup, and butter. Stir well to combine.
4. Add the flour mixture to the egg mixture and mix well.
5. Pour the dough into the greased pan. Bake for 45–50 minutes. Insert a toothpick into the loaf. If it comes out clean, it's done.

MAKES 1 LOAF, 10 SLICES

PER SERVING (1 SLICE)

Calories: 368

Calories from Fat: 249

Total Fat: 7g, 11%

Saturated Fat: 4g, 20%

Total Carb: 40g, 13%

Dietary Fiber: 2g, 8%

Sugars: 8g

Protein: 6g

Cholesterol: 70mg. 23%

Sodium: 213mg, 9%

Drizzled Cranberry-Almond Quick Bread

Baking with whole cranberries doesn't happen often enough. The tart pop of bright red cranberries lends incredible color and flavor to this simple quick bread. Try slathering hot slices with creamy almond butter and a drizzle of fresh honey for a truly delicious snack.

4 ½ tablespoons unsalted butter, melted

2 cups flour or **ALL-PURPOSE GLUTEN-FREE ALMOND FLOUR MIX (PAGE 27)**

½ cup light brown sugar

½ cup dark brown sugar

1 ½ teaspoons baking powder

1 teaspoon kosher salt

1 egg

¾ cup unsweetened almond milk

2 cups fresh or frozen whole cranberries

FOR THE ALMOND BUTTER LEMON DRIZZLE

3 tablespoons smooth almond butter

3 tablespoons raspberry honey or regular honey

1 ½ tablespoons lemon juice

1. Preheat the oven to 350°F. Butter a 9 × 5-inch loaf pan with ½ tablespoon of the melted butter. Flour the pan.

2. In a large bowl, sift together the flour, light brown sugar, dark brown sugar, baking powder, and salt.

3. In a medium bowl, beat the egg and add the remaining 4 tablespoons butter and the almond milk. Add the egg mixture to the flour mixture and mix well. Gently fold in the cranberries.

4. Pour the batter into the prepared pan. Bake for 1 hour and 15 minutes, until the edges are golden brown and a toothpick inserted into the center of the loaf comes out clean.

MAKES 1 LOAF, 8 SLICES

PER SERVING (1 SLICE)

Calories: 506

Calories from Fat: 238

Total Fat: 11g, 17%

Saturated Fat: 5g, 25%

Total Carb: 63g, 21%

Dietary Fiber: 3g, 12%

Sugars: 36g

Protein: 6g

Cholesterol: 39mg, 13%

Sodium: 430mg, 18%

5. Place the pan on a wire rack and let the bread cool for 30 minutes. Invert the bread onto the rack directly to finish cooling while you make the drizzle. When it's cool, transfer to a serving plate.

6. To make the drizzle, whisk together the almond butter, raspberry honey, and lemon juice. Drizzle it over the bread and let it soak in, about 3 minutes.

Classic Cinnamon Rolls Gone Gluten-Free

Quick-knead, no-rise, tons of protein and flavor! These incredible cinnamon rolls are made with almond flour and give those classic naughty cinnamon rolls a run for their money. While the instructions may seem somewhat complicated, it's important to be a little methodical with almond flour dough since it doesn't have the elasticity of a white or wheat dough. I've tried to walk you through every step to keep this recipe as fail proof as possible.

FOR THE ROLLS

4 tablespoons unsalted butter, room temperature

3 cups blanched almond flour

½ teaspoon kosher salt

¼ teaspoon baking soda

2 large eggs, room temperature

2 tablespoons raw honey

1 ½ teaspoons olive oil

FOR THE FILLING

½ cup raw honey

1 ½ teaspoons cinnamon

¼ teaspoon nutmeg

¼ teaspoon ground cloves

FOR THE ICING

1 ½ cups confectioners' sugar

3 tablespoons almond milk

MAKES 9 ROLLS

PER SERVING (1 ROLL)

Calories: 478

Calories from Fat: 257

Total Fat: 8g, 12%

Saturated Fat: 4g, 20%

Total Carb: 96g, 32%

Dietary Fiber: 2g, 8%

Sugars: 60g

Cholesterol: 62mg, 21%

Sodium: 187mg, 8%

Protein: 7g, 14%

1. Preheat the oven to 350°F. Line a rimmed cookie sheet with parchment paper.
2. Melt the butter in the microwave and set aside to cool for 5 minutes.
3. In a large bowl, combine the almond flour, salt, and baking soda. In a medium bowl, beat the eggs. Add the butter and

honey and stir well to combine. Add the wet ingredients to the dry mixture. Knead until the dough is smooth. Grease the outside of the dough with the olive oil. Refrigerate for 15 minutes.

4. Gently wet two large pieces of paper towel, so that they are just damp. Place on a cookie sheet and place a layer of parchment over them. *Note:* this is not the lined sheet you will bake the rolls on. (The paper towels will help to keep the parchment from sliding while rolling out the dough.) Place the dough on top of the parchment and place another piece of parchment on top of the dough.

5. Roll the dough out to approximately a 9 × 12-inch rectangle. Carefully spread the honey all over the dough using your hands or a soft spatula. Sprinkle the dough with the cinnamon, nutmeg, and cloves. Roll the dough up from the short end, and try to keep it as tight as possible. Cut into 1½ to 2-inch slices.

6. Place the rolls on the parchment-lined cookie sheet and bake for 10–15 minutes. The rolls are done when slightly brown and the middle is still a little soft. Place the pan on a wire cooking rack and let it cool for 15 minutes.

7. To make the icing, whisk the sugar and almond milk together. Pour into a zip-top plastic bag and snip off 1 corner of the bag. Pipe the icing over the cooled cinnamon rolls.

AB & J Quick Bread Bites

Nut butters and jelly are a classic combination. In this recipe for a simple, lightly sweetened almond butter quick bread, the flavors come together to create a delicious homemade bread that is perfect to pack in school lunches, easy to eat for breakfast, and wildly delicious for midnight snack attacks. To keep these bars as healthy as possible, use sugar-free, fruit-only preserves. Strawberry preserves are a favorite, but this bread would taste just as nice with little dollops of blackberry or raspberry jam.

D
gᴸ
gᴿ
pᴸ
vᵀ

MAKES 9 BARS

**PER SERVING
(1 BAR)**

Calories: 162

Calories from Fat: 79

Total Fat: 8.8g, 14%

Saturated Fat: 1.0g,
  5%

Total Carb: 16.9g, 6%

Dietary Fiber: 0.7g 3%

Sugars: 11.5g

Protein: 4.2g

Cholesterol: 36mg,
  12%

Sodium: 69mg, 3%

½ cup + 4 tablespoons creamy roasted almond butter

2 eggs

2 ½ tablespoons raw honey

1 tablespoon pure vanilla extract

¾ teaspoon baking powder

¼ teaspoon sea salt

6 tablespoons strawberry preserves

1. Preheat the oven to 350°F. Coat an 8 × 8-inch baking dish with nonstick cooking spray.
2. In a large bowl or stand mixer, beat together ½ cup of the almond butter, the eggs, honey, vanilla, baking powder, and salt until light and fluffy.
3. Spoon into the baking dish. Spoon half-tablespoon-size dollops of almond butter and strawberry preserves on top of the batter.
4. Bake for 11–15 minutes, or just until the edges are a light golden brown and the center of the bread has set. Remove from the oven and cool completely before slicing into 9 bars.

The Ultimate Thin Pizza Crust

This recipe really is the ultimate, because it's a pizza crust that everyone can eat! The recipe calls for flaxseed meal, which can be purchased in the gluten-free or vegan section of most health food stores. Two eggs or an equivalent amount of vegan egg replacer can substitute for the flaxseed meal. This recipe works best when rolled very thin. It cooks up light and crispy and tastes delicious when topped with all your favorite pizza toppings.

D
gL
gR
pL
VE
VT

⅔ cup flaxseed meal (or 2 eggs, or 1 teaspoon dry egg replacer mixed with 4 tablespoons water)

1 cup warm water

2 tablespoons coconut oil, butter, or Earth Balance, melted

2 cups blanched almond flour

7 tablespoons arrowroot powder

1 tablespoon baking powder

½ teaspoon salt

1. Preheat the oven to 400°F.
2. In a large bowl or stand mixer, whisk together the flaxseed meal, water, and oil. Keep beating until the mixture begins to thicken slightly. Add the almond flour, arrowroot powder, baking powder, and salt. Beat together until a well-mixed dough forms.
3. Separate the dough into two balls. Roll each ball of dough between two pieces of parchment until 12" in diameter, and about ⅛–¼" thick.
4. Bake for 12–15 minutes, or just until the edges of the dough turn a light golden brown.
5. Remove them from the oven, top with your favorite pizza toppings, and return to the oven to bake for 15–20 minutes more, until the edges of the crust are a light, golden brown.

MAKES 2 CRUSTS, 8 SERVINGS

PER SERVING (⅛ RECIPE)

Calories: 291

Calories from Fat: 187

Total Fat: 20.8g, 32%

Saturated Fat: 4.4g, 22%

Trans Fat: 0.0g

Total Carb: 13.9g, 5%

Dietary Fiber: 8.0g, 32%

Sugars—

Protein: 9.7g

Cholesterol: 0mg, 0%

Sodium: 164mg, 7%

5

Smoothies and Beverages

Almond milk and almond butter make truly creamy, sumptuous beverages. If you're looking to reduce or minimize dairy in your diet, almond milk can be stirred into your coffee, blended into smoothies, and made into milkshakes.

Add protein and flavor to your smoothies with a spoonful of almond butter. The flavor is surprisingly versatile in hot and cold drinks. It pairs beautifully with raspberries, strawberries, peaches, and even cocoa powder.

With recipes ranging from a piping-hot Vanilla Almond Steamer to a cool and frosty Peach Cobbler Smoothie, you'll find a slew of fun new ways to enjoy almond milk and almond butter in this chapter.

Become an Almond Barista

It's easy to make your favorite morning coffees with almond milk. Use it as you would cream and pour it straight into your favorite cup of coffee. Or blend like a barista with this quick guide to making morning coffees without dairy. Stevia makes a great, no-calorie sweetener, but use your favorite sweetener to turn any of these versions into your perfect cup.

Almond Milk Cappuccino

⅓ cup espresso, piping hot
⅓ cup vanilla almond milk

1. Pour the espresso into a large cappuccino cup.
2. Heat the almond milk in a small saucepan over medium heat. Use a hand blender to beat the milk until frothy.
3. Pour the almond milk into the espresso. Sweeten as desired. Serve immediately.

Almond Café Latte

⅓ cup espresso, piping hot
⅓ cup vanilla almond milk

1. Heat the almond milk in a saucepan and blend with a hand blender until frothy.
2. Pour the almond milk into the espresso, holding back the foam with a spoon. Pour the foam on top of the coffee and serve immediately.

Mocha

⅓ cup espresso, piping hot
⅓ cup chocolate almond milk
1 ½ teaspoons cocoa powder

1. Use chocolate almond milk instead of vanilla almond milk. Blend the cocoa powder into the mixture with a hand blender before pouring into your coffee cup.

MAKES 1 SERVING

**PER SERVING
(1 DRINK)**

Calories: 40
Calories from Fat: 20
Total Fat: 1g, 2%
Saturated Fat: 1g, 5%
Total Carb: 4g, 1%
Dietary Fiber: 0g, 0%
Sugars: 4g
Protein: 3g
Cholesterol: 5mg, 2%
Sodium: 50mg, 2%

Chai Latte

¼ cup chai concentrate

⅓ cup almond milk

1. In a saucepan, heat together the chai concentrate with the almond milk. Blend with a hand blender until frothy.
2. Pour into a coffee cup and serve immediately.

Pumpkin Spice Latte

⅓ cup espresso, piping hot

⅓ cup almond milk

1 tablespoon pumpkin puree

½ teaspoon pumpkin pie spice

1. Blend the pumpkin puree and pumpkin pie spice into the hot almond milk with a hand blender until frothy.
2. Pour mixture into espresso and serve immediately.

Vanilla Almond Steamer

This is the perfect just-before-bedtime drink. You can quickly turn this recipe into a feisty hot toddy by adding a shot of rum. If you've stored vanilla beans with the seeds already scraped, you can toss the empty pods into the almond milk as you heat it. You'll get little vanilla bean specks in your drink and lots of vanilla flavor.

4 cups vanilla almond milk

2 tablespoons pure maple syrup or raw honey

1 vanilla bean, scraped (optional)

¼ teaspoon cinnamon

1. In a large saucepan, heat the almond milk, maple syrup, and vanilla bean (if using) over medium-high heat until steaming.
2. Pour into mugs and sprinkle with cinnamon before serving.

MAKES 4 SERVINGS

PER SERVING (¼ RECIPE)

Calories: 146

Calories from Fat: 1

Total Fat: 5g, 8%

Saturated Fat: 3g, 15%

Total Carb: 17g, 6%

Dietary Fiber: 0g, 0%

Sugars: 16g

Protein: 9g

Cholesterol: 18mg, 6%

Sodium: 135mg, 6%

Double Dark Hot Cocoa

Cocoa powder and chocolate chips give twice the chocolately goodness to this rich, dark cocoa. Try serving it with peppermint sticks for a wintry kiss of mint!

4 cups vanilla almond milk
¼ cup unsweetened cocoa powder
¼ cup dark chocolate chips
¼ teaspoon sea salt
4 cinnamon sticks

1. Heat the almond milk in a medium saucepan over medium heat until gently boiling. Add the cocoa powder, chocolate chips, and salt.
2. Whisk until the chocolate is thoroughly combined and the drink is foamy (3–4 minutes).
3. Pour the hot chocolate into four mugs and serve with cinnamon sticks.

D **g^L** **g^R** **p^L** **v^E** **v^T**

MAKES 4 SERVINGS

PER SERVING
(¼ RECIPE)

Calories: 155
Calories from Fat: 48
Total Fat: 9g, 14%
Saturated Fat: 6g, 30%
Total Carb: 24g, 8%
Dietary Fiber: 3g, 12%
Sugars: 19g
Protein: 11g
Cholesterol: 18mg, 6%
Sodium: 311mg, 13%

Almond White Marshmallow Hot Cocoa

White chocolate and marshmallows go together beautifully when melted into steaming mugs of this yummy cocoa. Serve with biscotti or cookies for dipping and garnish with whipped cream, if desired.

4 cups vanilla almond milk

1 teaspoon cinnamon

1 cup white chocolate chips

¼ cup mini-marshmallows

1 tablespoon fresh mint

1. Heat the almond milk and cinnamon to a gentle boil in a medium saucepan over medium heat.
2. Add the white chocolate chips and gently whisk them into the almond milk until the chips melt (about 2–3 minutes).
3. Pour the hot white chocolate into four mugs. Top with the marshmallows and mint.

MAKES 6 SERVINGS

PER SERVING (⅙ RECIPE)

Calories: 214

Calories from Fat: 97

Total Fat: 10.8g, 17%

Saturated Fat: 5.5g, 28%

Total Carb: 27.8g, 9%

Dietary Fiber: 1.0g, 4%

Sugars: 26.7g

Protein: 2.4g

Cholesterol: 6mg, 2%

Sodium: 126mg, 5%

Almond Butter Hot Chocolate

Almond butter melts into a delicious, naturally sweetened cocoa made with pure ingredients. If you're eating paleo, use unsweetened almond milk and try swapping the maple syrup for stevia powder (and a big save on calories).

4 cups vanilla almond milk

4 tablespoons creamy roasted almond butter

1 tablespoon unsweetened cocoa powder

1 tablespoon pure maple syrup

1 teaspoon almond extract

1. In a small saucepan, whisk all the ingredients together over medium-high heat. Continue whisking as the mixture heats until it's smooth and frothy. Heat just until it's steaming but not boiling.
2. Pour into your favorite mugs and serve.

D gL gR vE vT

MAKES 6 SERVINGS

**PER SERVING
(⅙ RECIPE)**

Calories: 141

Calories from Fat: 70

Total Fat: 7.8g, 12%

Saturated Fat: 0.6g, 3%

Total Carb: 15.4g, 5%

Dietary Fiber: 1.4g, 5%

Sugars: 12.1g

Protein: 3.1g

Cholesterol: 0mg, 0%

Sodium: 101mg, 4%

Peppermint-Chocolate Mocha

Almond milk provides a perfectly creamy base for this hot, homemade mocha. Chocolate chips and peppermint extract turn a few shots of espresso into a mug that tastes a little like Christmas and a lot like delicious!

4 cups chocolate almond milk

½ teaspoon peppermint extract

1 cup espresso

¼ cup whipped cream or vegan cream

2 candy canes

1. Heat the almond milk, peppermint extract, and espresso together until steaming. Top with whipped cream and garnish with candy canes. Serve immediately.

D **gL** **gR** **VE** **VT**

MAKES 6 SERVINGS

**PER SERVING
(⅙ RECIPE)**

Calories: 164

Calories from Fat: 70

Total Fat: 7.8g, 12%

Saturated Fat: 3.4g, 17%

Total Carb: 21.7g, 7%

Dietary Fiber: 0.7g, 3%

Sugars: 18.7g

Protein: 1.6g

Cholesterol: 21mg, 7%

Sodium: 127mg, 5%

Orange Almond Whippy

Who says you need to head to the mall for a whippy orange drink?! Cut the dairy completely from this favorite childhood drink by blending almond milk with orange juice concentrate until it's foamy. You can also sweeten it with agave nectar, stevia, sugar, or grade-B maple syrup to taste.

1 cup orange juice concentrate

1 cup vanilla almond milk

2 cups ice

1 tablespoon honey, sugar, or pure maple syrup

2 teaspoons pure vanilla extract

1. Place all the ingredients in a blender and process until smooth.
2. Pour the orange drink into two chilled glasses and serve.

(D) (gL) (gR) (VE) (VT)

MAKES 2 SERVINGS

PER SERVING (½ RECIPE)

Calories: 193

Calories from Fat: 25

Total Fat: 2.8g, 4%

Saturated Fat: 0g

Total Carb: 38.5g, 13%

Dietary Fiber: 1.3g, 5%

Sugars: 24.8g

Protein: 2.1g

Cholesterol: 0mg, 0%

Sodium: 165mg, 7%

ABC Protein Shake

Start your day the healthy way with this bright pink shake that combines frozen Bing cherries with almond butter for a just-sweet-enough sipper. In this recipe, any creamy almond butter will do, but a raw, maple no-stir almond butter tastes best.

1 cup vanilla almond milk

1 ½ cups ice

1 cup pitted frozen cherries

2 tablespoons almond butter

1. Place all of the ingredients in a blender and process until smooth. Pour the smoothie into two glasses.

D
gL
gR
nL
vE
vT

MAKES 2 SERVINGS

PER SERVING (½ RECIPE)

Calories: 83

Calories from Fat: 96

Total Fat: 10g, 15%

Saturated Fat: 2g 10%

Total Carb: 36g 12%

Dietary Fiber: 4g 16%

Sugars: 31g

Protein: 9g

Cholesterol: 9mg 3%

Sodium: 99mg 4%

Chocolate Almond Smoothie

This is a decadent morning smoothie that almost tastes too good to be breakfast. The protein from the almond ingredients will help keep you going all morning. Health benefits aside, the mocha banana flavor here is so delicious, it makes a great dessert, too.

1 cup chocolate almond milk
¼ cup almond butter
1 tablespoon cocoa powder
1 tablespoon brewed espresso
1 banana, frozen

1. Place all the ingredients in a blender and process until smooth. Pour the smoothie into two glasses.

D
gL
gR
pL
vE
vT

MAKES 2 SERVINGS

**PER SERVING
(½ RECIPE)**

Calories: 280
Calories from Fat: 179
Total Fat: 19.9g, 31%
Saturated Fat: 1.9g, 10%
Total Carb: 22.1g, 7%
Dietary Fiber: 4.0g, 16%
Sugars: 7.3g
Protein: 8.8g
Cholesterol: 0mg, 0%
Sodium: 92mg, 4%

Peach Cobbler Smoothie

Peaches and vanilla almond milk plus a smidgen of almond butter make this rich, hearty smoothie a perfect start to any morning routine. Sweeten, if desired, with stevia, honey, or a smidgen of maple syrup.

1 cup frozen peaches

½ cup vanilla almond milk

2 tablespoons raw almond butter

1 teaspoon pumpkin pie spice

1 teaspoon pure vanilla extract

½ tablespoon sliced almonds for garnish (optional)

1. In a blender, puree the peaches, almond milk, almond butter, pumpkin pie spice, and vanilla until smooth.
2. Pour into two glasses. Sprinkle with sliced almonds, if desired.

D
GL
GR
PL
VE
VT

MAKES 2 SERVINGS

**PER SERVING
(½ RECIPE)**

Calories: 267

Calories from Fat: 91

Total Fat: 10g, 15%

Saturated Fat: 1g, 5%

Total Carb: 40g, 13%

Dietary Fiber: 4g, 16%

Sugars: 35g

Protein: 6g

Cholesterol: 5mg, 2%

Sodium: 73mg, 3%

Banana Almond Butter Protein Blast

If you like cookie dough, you're going to love this almond butter smoothie. The final whipped drink tastes like banana almond cookie dough with bits of chocolate chips blended in but doesn't contain a single ounce of added sugar, thanks to the natural sweetness of the bananas.

D
GL
GR
PL
VE
VT

2 frozen bananas, chopped into 2-inch pieces

1½ cups vanilla almond milk

¼ cup almond butter

⅛ teaspoon kosher salt

¼ cup dark chocolate chips (if vegan, make sure your chips have no animal ingredients)

1. Place the bananas, almond milk, almond butter, and salt in a blender and process until smooth.
2. Put the chocolate in a small, clean microwavable bowl and microwave on high for 1 minute. Stir the chips. If the chocolate still needs to melt, microwave it in 10 second intervals until it's completely melted.
3. Pour the smoothie into two glasses and top with the melted chocolate.

MAKES 2 SERVINGS

PER SERVING (½ RECIPE)

Calories: 418

Calories from Fat: 210

Total Fat: 23.3g, 36%

Saturated Fat: 4.3g, 21%

Total Carb: 50.5g, 17%

Dietary Fiber: 4.7g, 19%

Sugars: 29.9g

Protein: 9.4g

Cholesterol: 0mg, 0%

Sodium: 1,239mg, 52%

Strawberry Almond Smoothie

Strawberries and almonds taste scrumptious together, and this simple smoothie is a perfect way to start the morning. Boost the almond flavor with a half-teaspoon of almond extract. Feel free to swap in frozen blueberries for an equally delicious sipper.

1 ½ cups + 1 tablespoon frozen strawberries
1 ½ cups almond milk
½ cup orange juice

1. Combine the 1 ½ cups frozen strawberries, almond milk, and orange juice in a blender and process until smooth.
2. Roughly chop the tablespoon of strawberries.
3. Pour the smoothies into two glasses. Top with the chopped strawberries. Serve immediately.

D
gL
gR
nL
vE
vT

MAKES 2 SERVINGS

**PER SERVING
(½ RECIPE)**

Calories: 349
Calories from Fat: 300
Total Fat: 4g, 6%
Saturated Fat: 2g,
  10%
Total Carb: 77g, 26%
Dietary Fiber: 6g, 24%
Sugars: 68g
Protein: 9g
Cholesterol: 14mg, 5%
Sodium: 104mg, 4%

Coconut-Almond Green Smoothie

This bright, creamy smoothie uses coconut cream, which can be purchased on-line or can often be found near the coconut milk in most health food grocers. If you're unable to find it, swap in ½ cup coconut milk yogurt instead. The addition of kale gives a nutrient boost, and you won't even be able to taste it!

½ cup coconut cream

6 tablespoons raw maple almond butter

2 cups kale, chopped

1 ½ cups vanilla almond milk

1 cup ice cubes

1. Place all the ingredients in a blender. Blend until smooth.
2. Pour into two glasses and serve immediately.

D
gL
gR
pL
vE
vT

MAKES 4 SERVINGS

**PER SERVING
(¼ RECIPE)**

Calories: 238

Calories from Fat: 188

Total Fat: 20.9g, 32%

Saturated Fat: 7.6g, 38%

Total Carb: 9.2g, 3%

Dietary Fiber: 2.2g, 9%

Sugars: 1.0g

Protein: 6.9g

Cholesterol: 0mg, 0%

Sodium: 21mg, 1%

6

Snacks, Appetizers, and Sides

A schmear of almond butter on a golden apple is nice, but there are so many other ways to enjoy almond products as a snack, starter, or side dish. This chapter gives you dozens of ideas, from everyday to elegant—treats you can toss out as afterschool snacks, or beautiful two-bite appetizers that will complement any cocktail party.

With more and more allergen-free eaters, and more and more people seeking healthy indulgences, these starters are sure to be a welcome addition to parties and picnic tables. The ingredients are mostly whole and fresh. Gluten-free and vegan options abound, and many of the recipes are kid-friendly for children who may otherwise turn up their noses at something that isn't quite the same as their beloved peanut butter.

Paleo eaters are encouraged to serve the crostini recipes on slices of almond bread, nut thin crackers, or slices of cucumber. We can't have our fellow no-wheat foodies living without these divine treats!

Almond Crunch Crackers

Making crackers at home is surprisingly easy. This is the simplest almond cracker you can make, calling for just four ingredients. The crackers bake up thin and crispy and pair beautifully with savory dips and spreads.

2 cups blanched almond flour

1 ½ tablespoons avocado or olive oil (or grapeseed, if you're not following a paleo diet)

1 ½ tablespoons water

1 teaspoon coarsely ground sea salt

1. Preheat the oven to 350°F.
2. In a large bowl, stir together the almond flour, oil, water, and ½ teaspoon of the salt until a thick dough forms.
3. Press the dough into a ball and place it between two large pieces of parchment paper. Roll the dough with a rolling pin until ¹⁄₁₆ inch thick. Use a pizza cutter or pastry cutter to slice the dough into squares.
4. Carefully transfer the parchment with the cut crackers to a baking sheet. Sprinkle with the remaining sea salt.
5. Bake for 6–9 minutes, or just until the crackers are light golden brown.
6. Remove from the oven and cool completely before serving.

D **gL** **gR** **pL** **VE** **VT**

MAKES ABOUT 48 CRACKERS

PER SERVING (3 CRACKERS)

Calories: 95

Calories from Fat: 72

Total Fat: 8.0g, 12%

Saturated Fat: 0.7g, 3%

Total Carb: 3.0g, 1%

Dietary Fiber: 1.5g, 6%

Protein: 3.0g

Cholesterol: 0mg, 0%

Sodium: 103mg, 4%

Go gourmet with your almond crackers!

Turn this recipe for basic Almond Crunch Crackers into a variety of incredible flavors. Here are a few easy mix-ins that will turn this basic recipe into a gourmet treat.

SAVORY. Need crackers that pair nicely with cheese plates, savory spreads, and antipasto platters? These delicious versions are great for any occasion.

> **Cheddar.** Add 1 tablespoon nutritional yeast to the dough, increase the water by ½ teaspoon.

> **Rosemary.** Add 1 tablespoon dried rosemary to the dough.

> **Sesame.** Add 1 tablespoon black sesame seeds to the dough.

> **Fresh Herb.** Stir 1 tablespoon fresh, finely chopped herbs (sage, parsley, oregano, and/or tarragon) into the dough before rolling out.

> **Black Pepper.** Add ½ teaspoon freshly ground black pepper to the dough before slicing and baking.

SWEET. For dessert dips and sweet spreads, there's nothing like a crunchy cracker to go along with them. Try serving these crackers alongside apple dips or with mild, soft cheeses for a fun treat.

> **Honey.** Add 1 tablespoon honey to the dough and reduce the oil and water by ½ tablespoon each.

> **Cinnamon Sugar.** Sprinkle the tops of the cut crackers with 1 tablespoon cinnamon sugar before baking.

> **Chocolate.** Add 2 tablespoons cocoa powder to the dough, and increase the oil and water by 1 teaspoon each.

Almond Butter Hummus

Hummus has grown in popularity over the years, and for good reason—it's delicious! This recipe adds creamy almond butter for a touch of natural sweetness and tons of flavor. Raw or roasted almond butter works equally well in this hummus. This recipe calls for roasted garlic, which is usually found in the olive bar, near the deli section of most grocery stores. If you can't find it, feel free to omit it.

2 cloves roasted garlic

1 (15-ounce) can garbanzo beans, drained and rinsed

¼ cup + 2 tablespoons olive oil

3 tablespoons almond butter

3 tablespoons lemon juice

¼ teaspoon salt

1 tablespoon finely chopped flat-leaf parsley

¼ teaspoon smoked paprika

1. Place the garlic, garbanzo beans, ¼ cup of the oil, the almond butter, lemon juice, and salt in a food processor fitted with a metal blade. Pulse to desired consistency. Add more salt if desired.
2. Garnish with a sprinkling of fresh chopped parsley and paprika.

MAKES 16 SERVINGS

PER SERVING (¹⁄₁₆ RECIPE)

Calories: 134

Calories from Fat: 30

Total Fat: 5g, 8%

Saturated Fat: 0g, 0%

Total Carb: 19g, 6%

Dietary Fiber: 4g, 16%

Sugars: 1g

Protein: 5g

Cholesterol: 0mg, 0%

Sodium: 349mg, 15%

Creamy Almond Butter and Honey Apple Dip

Quick and easy to toss together for snacking, almond butter and honey mixed with yogurt make a great dip for apples, strawberries, or slices of bananas and kiwi. Little cubes of banana bread also pair well with this yummy dip.

3 tablespoons creamy almond butter
4 ounces cream cheese
¼ cup Greek yogurt
2 tablespoons honey
¼ teaspoon apple pie spice
2 Granny Smith apples, cored and cut into ½-inch slices.

1. Whip the almond butter, cream cheese, yogurt, and honey together in a medium bowl and chill for 1 hour to let the flavors meld.
2. Sprinkle with the apple pie spice before serving. Serve with the apple slices for dipping.

MAKES 8 SERVINGS

PER SERVING (⅛ RECIPE)

Calories: 121
Calories from Fat: 72
Total Fat: 8.0g, 12%
Saturated Fat: 3.3g, 17%
Total Carb: 12.2g, 4%
Dietary Fiber: 1.9g, 7%
Sugars: 9.4g
Protein: 2.4g
Cholesterol: 16mg, 5%
Sodium: 63mg, 3%

Enlightened Artichoke Dip

Everyone will love diving into this creamy, delicious spinach-artichoke dip. Perfect for serving with **ALMOND CRUNCH CRACKERS (PAGE 90),** *fresh bell pepper slices, carrot sticks, and celery, this healthy version is made without cheese, dairy milk, or butter. Most importantly, it's not just good for you, it's downright delicious! This recipe works best when made in a high-speed, industrial-strength blender like a Vitamix, but can also be mixed in a food processor.*

½ cup unsweetened almond milk

½ cup raw cashews

2 tablespoons lemon juice

1 teaspoon dried ground mustard

1 tablespoon nutritional yeast (optional)

1 clove garlic

½ teaspoon sea salt

1 ½ cups canned artichoke hearts

1 ½ cups fresh spinach

1. Preheat the oven to 400°F.
2. Place the almond milk, cashews, and lemon juice in a blender. Blend until the mixture turns a light, creamy consistency.
3. Add the ground mustard, nutritional yeast (if using), garlic, and salt to the blender. Mix until pureed.
4. Add the artichoke hearts and spinach, and blend on low speed, just until they're chopped into the mixture.
5. Transfer to an 8 × 8-inch baking dish and bake until the mixture is bubbling, about 20–25 minutes.
6. Remove and cool slightly before serving.

MAKES 6 SERVINGS

**PER SERVING
(⅙ RECIPE)**

Calories: 134

Calories from Fat: 52

Total Fat: 5g, 8%

Saturated Fat: 0g, 0%

Total Carb: 19g, 6%

Dietary Fiber: 4g, 16%

Sugars: 1g

Protein: 5g

Cholesterol: 0mg, 0%

Sodium: 349mg, 15%

White Bean and Roasted Red Pepper Spread

Whether you're dipping into it with crackers or schmearing it on crostini or celery sticks, this healthy spread is delicious. Mildly sweetened from the roasted red peppers with a subtle kick of heat, it's a great addition to any party platter and makes a fine midafternoon snack, too.

D
gL
VE
VT

1 (15-ounce can) Great Northern beans, drained

3 tablespoons creamy almond butter

2 strips roasted red bell pepper

1 clove garlic

1 tablespoon hot sesame oil

¼ cup avocado, grapeseed, or olive oil

2 tablespoons chopped fresh cilantro

1. Place the beans, almond butter, pepper strips, garlic, sesame oil, and avocado oil in a food processor or industrial-strength blender. Puree until very smooth, about 2–3 minutes.
2. Serve with a drizzle of olive oil and fresh cilantro sprinkled on top. Store covered in the fridge for up to 1 week.

MAKES 6 SERVINGS

PER SERVING (⅙ RECIPE)

Calories: 138

Calories from Fat: 100

Total Fat: 5g, 8%

Saturated Fat: 1g, 5%

Total Carb: 18g, 6%

Dietary Fiber: 5g, 20%

Sugars: 1g

Protein: 6g

Cholesterol: 0mg, 0%

Sodium: 5mg, 0%

Acorn Squash Crostini

Crostini with this creamy squash topping make a beautiful autumn appetizer, but they can also be topped with fresh garden tomatoes and basil for a summertime snack. Paleo eaters will enjoy the puree on **ALMOND CRUNCH CRACKERS (PAGE 90)**. *If you're a goat cheese lover, a smidgen of goat cheese crumbled on top tastes divine.*

D
GL
VE
VT

MAKES 6 SERVINGS

**PER SERVING
(⅙ RECIPE)**

Calories: 272
Calories from Fat: 39
Total Fat: 8g, 12%
Saturated Fat: 1g, 5%
Total Carb: 41g, 14%
Dietary Fiber: 3g, 12%
Sugars: 2g
Protein: 10g
Cholesterol: 0mg, 0%
Sodium: 554mg, 23%

1 small acorn or butternut squash
1 tablespoon olive, grapeseed, or avocado oil
½ teaspoon salt
¼ teaspoon freshly ground pepper
2 cloves roasted garlic
3 tablespoons roasted almond butter
1 tablespoon chopped fresh sage
20 slices baguette (gluten-free, if desired), toasted

1. Preheat the oven to 400°F.
2. Slice the acorn squash in half lengthwise and place it cut-side up on a parchment-lined baking sheet. Drizzle with oil and sprinkle with salt and pepper.
3. Bake for 35–45 minutes, or until the squash is very soft and tender when pierced with a fork. Remove from oven and allow to cool.
4. Scoop the meat from the center of each squash.
5. Transfer to a food processor or industrial-strength blender. Add the roasted garlic and almond butter to the squash and pulse until pureed.
6. Spread onto the toasted baguette slices and garnish with the chopped sage.

Melty Bacon-Almond Crostini

This combination of ingredients may seem peculiar, but you've gotta try it. For these crostini, the savory topping is baked atop the baguette slices until it's toasty and golden brown. Prep the crostini before a party and pop them in the oven for baking whenever you're ready to have a hot and tasty appetizer.

D
gL
gR
VE
VT

1 tablespoon finely chopped shallot

3 tablespoons creamy roasted almond butter

3 tablespoons mayonnaise or vegan mayo

2 tablespoons bacon bits or vegan bacon bits

⅔ cup shredded Monterey Jack or soy cheese

16 baguette slices (gluten-free, if desired)

2 tablespoons chopped scallions

1. Preheat the oven to 400°F.
2. In a medium bowl, stir together the shallot, almond butter, mayonnaise, bacon bits, and cheese. Spoon the spread on top of the baguette slices.
3. Place them on a parchment-lined baking sheet and bake for 10–12 minutes, or until the cheese is melted and light golden brown.
4. Remove from the oven and garnish with chopped scallions.

MAKES 8 SERVINGS

PER SERVING
(⅛ RECIPE)

Calories: 240

Calories from Fat: 58

Total Fat: 12g, 18%

Saturated Fat: 3g, 15%

Total Carb: 24g, 8%

Dietary Fiber: 2g, 8%

Sugars: 1g

Protein: 9g

Cholesterol: 10mg, 3%

Sodium: 337mg, 14%

Cucumber Butter Bites

I'm a firm believer in having a few recipes up your sleeve that can be whipped up in seconds and served with a flourish. This recipe is one of those. It's healthy, crazy quick to make, and handy for offering to unexpected guests. Pair it with white wine for a nice cocktail appetizer or serve it as an afterschool snack.

1 cucumber, sliced into ¼-inch slices
¼ cup almond butter
¼ cup fresh halved cherries or pomegranate arils
3 tablespoons sliced almonds
1 teaspoon fresh mint leaves, finely chopped
½ teaspoon coarse sea salt

1. Arrange the cucumbers on a serving platter.
2. Place the almond butter in a plastic zip-top bag. Snip a corner from the bag, and pipe ½ teaspoon of the almond butter onto each cucumber slice.
3. Sprinkle with the cherries, almonds, and mint leaves. Sprinkle with salt and serve immediately.

Ⓓ Ⓖ ⒼⓇ Ⓟ ⓋⒺ ⓋⓉ

MAKES 6 SERVINGS

PER SERVING
(⅙ RECIPE)

Calories: 95

Calories from Fat: 67

Total Fat: 7.4g, 11%

Saturated Fat: 0.7g, 3%

Total Carb: 5.2g, 2%

Dietary Fiber: 1.1g, 5%

Sugars: 0.9g

Protein: 3.3g

Cholesterol: 0mg, 0%

Sodium: 161mg, 7%

Almond Cream Cheese Ball

Gluten-free graham crackers and apple slices make fun dippers into this unique twist on the classic savory cheese ball. Try serving it before Thanksgiving dinner or offer it as a party snack.

D
gL
gR
vE
vT

1 (8-ounce) package Neufchâtel cheese or vegan cream cheese
½ cup creamy, no-stir almond butter
¼ cup honey, brown sugar, maple syrup, or agave nectar
½ teaspoon cinnamon
¾ cup chopped walnuts

1. In a medium bowl or stand mixer, beat together the cream cheese, almond butter, maple syrup, and cinnamon until smooth.
2. Spoon the mixture into a large piece of plastic wrap, form it into a ball, and refrigerate it for 20 minutes.
3. Roll it in the walnuts just before serving.

MAKES 12 SERVINGS

PER SERVING (¹/₁₂ RECIPE)

Calories: 150
Calories from Fat: 118
Total Fat: 13.1g, 20%
Saturated Fat: 2.6g, 13%
Total Carb: 3.9g, 1%
Dietary Fiber: 1.0g, 4%
Sugars: 1.3g
Protein: 5.9g
Cholesterol: 9mg, 3%
Sodium: 89mg, 4%

Salted Almond Butter Popcorn

A little bit sweet, a little bit savory, this quick snack is perfect for midafternoon munchies. It also makes for a trendy appetizer at cocktail parties. If you're lucky enough to live near a grocery that sells gourmet salts, try sprinkling smoked sea salt for a truly scrumptious flavor addition.

D
gL
vE
vT

6 cups popped popcorn
2 tablespoons roasted almond butter
1 teaspoon honey or pure maple syrup
1 tablespoon coconut oil
½ teaspoon coarse sea salt

1. Place the popcorn in a large bowl.
2. In a small saucepan over medium heat, melt the almond butter, honey, and coconut oil together until bubbly. Stir and allow it to boil for about 45 seconds.
3. Drizzle the mixture over the popcorn. Immediately sprinkle with sea salt.

MAKES 12 SERVINGS

PER SERVING (¹/₁₂ RECIPE)

Calories: 27
Calories from Fat: 12
Total Fat: 2g, 3%
Saturated Fat: 1g, 5%
Total Carb: 1g, 0%
Dietary Fiber: 0g, 0%
Sugars: 1g
Protein: 1g
Cholesterol: 0mg, 0%
Sodium: 102mg, 4%

Mashed Cauliflower

Almond milk mixes into this mashed cauliflower, creating a low-carb side dish that tastes just like mashed potatoes. This recipe works as a great base for any number of variations. Feel free to fold in bacon bits, chopped chives, parsley, shredded cheddar—anything you'd stir into mashed potatoes will taste great when added to this scrumptious side dish.

D
gL
gR
pL
vE
vT

1 large cauliflower

2 cloves roasted garlic (optional)

1 tablespoon nutritional yeast, butter, or Earth Balance

¼ cup unsweetened almond milk

½ teaspoon salt

½ teaspoon coarsely ground pepper

1. Cut the florets from the cauliflower.
2. Place the cauliflower florets in a large pot and cover them with water. Cover the pot and bring the water to a boil over high heat. Allow the cauliflower to boil until very tender, about 25 minutes.
3. Drain the cauliflower completely in a strainer, transfer to a large bowl, and add the garlic (if using), nutritional yeast, almond milk, salt, and pepper to the bowl.
4. Use a hand blender to puree. If you don't have a hand blender, puree half of the cauliflower with the roasted garlic and almond milk in a blender, then transfer it to a stand mixer and beat the pureed cauliflower and remaining cauliflower together until it's reached the texture of mashed potatoes.

MAKES 4 SERVINGS

**PER SERVING
(¼ RECIPE)**

Calories: 79

Calories from Fat: 2

Total Fat: 2g, 3%

Saturated Fat: 0g, 0%

Total Carb: 14g, 5%

Dietary Fiber: 6g, 24%

Sugars: 5g

Protein: 6g

Cholesterol: 1mg, 0%

Sodium: 370mg, 15%

Creamy Pepper Gravy

Here's a classic southern cream gravy, without the cream. Try serving this **CREAMY PEPPER GRAVY OVER THE MASHED CAULIFLOWER (PAGE 101)**, or stir in sausage or vegan sausage crumbles and serve over the **MILE-HIGH BIS-CUITS (PAGE 53)** for a hearty breakfast of biscuits and gravy. This gravy works well over salmon, chicken, and steak, and pairs nicely with sautéed mushrooms, too.

(D)
(GL)
(GR)
(DL)
(VE)
(VT)

1 tablespoon butter or Earth Balance
1 ½ cups almond milk
2 tablespoons arrowroot powder
½ teaspoon salt
2 teaspoons freshly ground pepper

1. In a skillet, heat the butter over medium heat until it's melted.
2. Whisk in ½ cup of the almond milk and arrowroot powder, then whisk in the remaining almond milk and heat the mixture just until the gravy begins to thicken.
3. Remove from the heat, stir in the salt and pepper.

MAKES 4 SERVINGS

**PER SERVING
(¼ RECIPE)**

Calories: 90
Calories from Fat: 81
Total Fat: 5g, 8%
Saturated Fat: 3g, 15%
Total Carb: 9g, 3%
Dietary Fiber: 0g, 0%
Sugars: 4g
Protein: 4g
Cholesterol: 14mg, 5%
Sodium: 367mg, 15%

Almond Flour Polenta

Gluten-free and low-carb eaters often have to live without some of the most comforting side dishes around. But life doesn't have to be lived without polenta! Though traditional polenta is made with boiled cornmeal, almond flour makes a quick and simple version that has the same texture as polenta—and the taste is just as good. Polenta tastes great wherever you'd serve rice or mashed potatoes and is incredible when topped with fresh tomatoes, marinara, and savory compotes.

1 cup blanched almond flour

1 cup water

½ teaspoon salt

1 tablespoon butter or Earth Balance (optional)

2 tablespoons nutritional yeast (or ¼ cup shredded parmesan cheese)

½ teaspoon freshly ground pepper

1. In a medium saucepan, stir together the almond flour, water, and salt. Whisk until well combined, then bring the mixture to a boil over medium heat. As it begins to boil, resume whisking the mixture until it starts to thicken, about 2 minutes.
2. Remove from the heat and whisk in the butter (if using), nutritional yeast, and pepper.
3. Serve as a side dish with chicken, fish, or Italian dishes.

MAKES 4 SERVINGS

PER SERVING (¼ RECIPE)

Calories: 146

Calories from Fat: 140

Total Fat: 3g, 5%

Saturated Fat: 2g, 10%

Total Carb: 25g, 8%

Dietary Fiber: 1g, 4%

Sugars: 0g

Protein: 4g

Cholesterol: 8mg, 3%

Sodium: 318mg, 13%

Roasted Cinnamon Squash

This side dish is easy to toss together and bakes while you prep dinner, so it makes it easy to add a pop of colorful, flavorful veggies to any meal. If you're in a hurry and don't have time to peel a whole squash, look for frozen cubes of butternut squash in the freezer section. It'll take just 20 minutes to bake and gives the same great flavor as fresh squash. Serve this side dish with any chicken, fish, or steak meal or atop salad greens with a balsamic vinaigrette and a sprinkle of toasted pine nuts.

D **gL** **gR** **pL** **VE** **VT**

MAKES 4 SERVINGS

**PER SERVING
(¼ RECIPE)**

Calories: 151
Calories from Fat: 140
Total Fat: 10g, 15%
Saturated Fat: 1g, 5%
Total Carb: 15g, 5%
Dietary Fiber: 3g, 12%
Sugars: 9g
Protein: 4g
Cholesterol: 0mg, 0%
Sodium: 515mg, 21%

1 large butternut squash or 2 medium acorn squashes

½ shallot, finely diced

4 tablespoons avocado, grapeseed, or olive oil

2 tablespoons almond butter

1 tablespoon soy sauce, tamari, or Bragg Liquid Aminos

¼ teaspoon cinnamon

1 cup chopped dino kale

½ teaspoon salt

¼ cup sliced almonds, toasted (optional)

2 tablespoons raw honey or maple syrup (optional)

1. Preheat the oven to 400°F.
2. Cut the peel from the squash, remove the seeds, and slice the squash meat into bite-size cubes.
3. In a large bowl, whisk together the shallot, oil, almond butter, soy sauce, and cinnamon.
4. Toss the squash and kale in the almond butter mixture, then place it in a parchment-lined 9 × 13-inch baking dish. Sprinkle with the salt.
5. Cover and bake for 45 minutes, or until the squash is tender.
6. Remove from the oven and serve topped with almonds and a drizzle of honey or maple syrup, if desired.

Marinated Spicy Kale Salad

Curly or dino kale drenched in a hearty almond butter dressing is a truly tasty combination. The fully grown bunches of kale are tough and stand up to marinating (though you'll want to cut out and remove the stems before tossing the kale into this recipe). Baby kale, however, is tender and will wilt into a soggy mess if used in this recipe, so stick with the bigger bunches for the best results.

(D) (GL) (GR) (DL) (VE) (VT)

5 cups chopped curly or dino kale leaves

FOR THE DRESSING
3 tablespoons lemon juice
¼ cup olive oil
1 shallot, finely diced
2 tablespoons almond butter
1 teaspoon whole-grain mustard
½ teaspoon cayenne
½ teaspoon tamari, soy sauce, or Bragg Liquid Aminos
1 teaspoon raw honey or agave nectar
½ teaspoon salt
¼ teaspoon freshly ground pepper

1. Place the kale in a large bowl.
2. Whisk together the lemon juice, olive oil, shallot, almond butter, mustard, cayenne, tamari, and honey in a small bowl. Season with salt and pepper.
3. Drizzle the dressing over the kale, cover the bowl, place it in the fridge, and allow it to marinate for up to 1 hour before serving.

MAKES 4 SERVINGS

**PER SERVING
(¼ RECIPE)**

Calories: 141
Calories from Fat: 107
Total Fat: 11.9g, 18%
Saturated Fat: 1.6g,
   8%
Total Carb: 7.8g, 3%
Dietary Fiber: 1.4g,
   6%
Sugars: 1.1g
Protein: 3.1g
Cholesterol: 0mg, 0%
Sodium: 264mg, 11%

7

Sandwiches

Almond butter does more than stand in for peanut butter on sandwiches. It pairs with a surprising number of sweet and savory flavors and adds a mild, naturally sweet nuttiness to everything from breakfast sandwiches to hearty dinner hoagies. In this chapter, you'll discover some recipes with familiar flavor combinations, some with surprising ingredient pairings.

Everyone loves the classic combinations (almond butter with raspberry jam is familiar and likeable). Although some eaters pull out a nose-crinkle at the slightest tiptoe into unfamiliar-flavor land, these sandwiches have been kid and grown-up tested and approved. You might not think to mix almond butter and grilled cheese together, but it makes a surprisingly scrumptious sammy. Men, women, picky tots, and teens all devoured bite after bite and begged for more.

Try the Thai-Style Almond Butter Sandwich for a healthy sandwich full of fresh, crunchy veggie flavor anytime you need a lunch that switches up the same-old. Though the combination sounds odd, it's a fun way to break the sweet almond butter sandwich routine. There are plenty of other fun, new ways to eat almond butter on bread in this chapter. Each is an easy way to boost your almond intake, while serving up simple food that's positively scrumptious.

Open-Faced Almond Butter and Banana Sandwiches

Almond butter and bananas go together deliciously! Use raw or roasted almond butter in this easy, open-face "sandwich." Try serving it for breakfast or as an after-school snack for a quick, yummy treat full of protein and potassium.

1 banana, sliced in half lengthwise

4 tablespoons almond butter

1 tablespoon toasted coconut

1 tablespoon chopped pecans

1 tablespoon dried cranberries

2 tablespoons honey or pure maple syrup

1. Spread the almond butter over the cut side of each banana.
2. Sprinkle the coconut, pecans, and cranberries over the almond butter. Drizzle with honey or maple syrup and serve immediately.

D **gL** **gR** **pL** **vE** **vT**

MAKES 2 SERVINGS

**PER SERVING
(½ RECIPE)**

Calories: 333

Calories from Fat: 194

Total Fat: 19g, 29%

Saturated Fat: 2g, 10%

Total Carb: 40g, 13%

Dietary Fiber: 5g, 20%

Sugars: 29g

Protein: 7g

Cholesterol: 0mg, 0%

Sodium: 63mg, 3%

Open-Faced Almond Butter and Bacon Sammy

If you're looking for a quick, unusual breakfast, this absurdly simple recipe is about to become a new favorite. Though it's likely you haven't thought to pair these flavors, they come together perfectly, making a quick meal that's tasty to the very last nibble.

D
gL
VE
VT

2 slices cinnamon-swirl bread (gluten-free, if desired), toasted

4 tablespoons almond butter

1 Granny Smith apple, cored and sliced thin

4 slices bacon, cooked and coarsely chopped

1 tablespoon avocado, grapeseed, or olive oil

¼ teaspoon salt

¼ teaspoon freshly ground pepper

1. Spread the almond butter on the toast. Place the apple slices and bacon on top.
2. Drizzle them with oil and sprinkle with salt and pepper. Serve immediately.

MAKES 2 SERVINGS

**PER SERVING
(½ RECIPE)**

Calories: 578

Calories from Fat: 377

Total Fat: 41.9g, 64%

Saturated Fat: 8.1g, 41%

Total Carb: 28.7g, 10%

Dietary Fiber: 5.6g, 22%

Sugars: 10.1g

Protein: 24.5g

Cholesterol: 42mg, 14%

Sodium: 1301mg, 54%

Almond Grilled Elvis

Elvis's mama would have been so proud. Here I've put an almond spin on one of The King's famous food combos—peanut butter, bacon, and bananas—by swapping almond butter for peanut butter. So good, this sandwich will have you howling like a hound dog!

2 tablespoons almond butter

4 slices bread (gluten-free if desired)

1 large ripe banana, sliced vertically into four thin pieces

4 slices regular or vegan bacon, cooked

2 tablespoons organic honey or pure maple syrup

2 tablespoons unsalted butter, softened, or Earth Balance

1. Spread 1 tablespoon almond butter on 2 slices of bread and top each with 2 pieces of banana and 2 slices of bacon. Drizzle 1 tablespoon honey on each.
2. Spread ½ tablespoon of butter on the 2 remaining slices of bread and place them buttered side up on the slices with bananas and bacon.
3. Melt the remaining tablespoon of butter or Earth Balance in a large skillet over medium low heat.
4. Cook the sandwiches until golden brown and crispy, approximately 3 minutes. Flip and cook on the other side for an additional 3 minutes.

D
gL
gR
vE
vT

MAKES 2 SANDWICHES

PER SERVING (1 SANDWICH)

Calories: 452

Calories from Fat: 167

Total Fat: 18.5g, 28%

Saturated Fat: 1.8g, 9%

Total Carb: 71.3g, 24%

Dietary Fiber: 4.8g, 19%

Sugars: 51.1g

Protein: 8.4g

Cholesterol: 0mg, 0%

Sodium: 3mg, 0%

Vegaroo Almond Butter Wrap

Almond butter sauce brings out the flavor of fresh veggies in this veggie-packed wrap. Paleo eaters can serve the filling in a lettuce wrap.

1 tablespoon almond butter

1 tablespoon olive oil

1 tablespoon rice vinegar

1 teaspoon horseradish mustard

¼ teaspoon kosher salt

Freshly ground pepper

2 gluten-free wheat tortillas

1 cup raw spinach, chopped

½ cup broccoli florets, chopped

¼ cup shredded carrot

¼ cup alfalfa sprouts

1 scallion (white and green parts), chopped

1 small white radish, sliced

1. For the dressing, whisk together the almond butter, oil, vinegar, mustard, and salt. Add pepper to taste.
2. Divide the vegetables between the two tortillas and top with the dressing. Roll each tortilla into a burrito and serve.

(D) (g) (p) (VT)

MAKES 2 WRAPS

PER SERVING (1 WRAP)

Calories: 266

Calories from Fat: 128

Total Fat: 14.2g, 22%

Saturated Fat: 1.4g, 7%

Total Carb: 29.4g, 10%

Dietary Fiber: 3.9g, 16%

Sugars: 1.3g

Protein: 5.2g

Cholesterol: 0mg, 0%

Sodium: 521mg, 22%

Almond-Strawberry Spicy Cheddar Quesadilla

Elevate the traditional cheese quesadilla into a gourmet eat with the addition of cheddar and fresh strawberries. If the combination seems odd, you're about to be surprised. The creamy cheddar, rich almond butter, strawberries, and chopped fresh jalapeño work together to create a totally crave-able flavor. For a dairy-free treat, replace the cheddar with vegan cheddar cheese.

2 tablespoons almond butter

2 tablespoons sour cream or vegan sour cream

4 tortillas (gluten-free if desired)

8–10 fresh strawberries, trimmed and sliced

½ fresh jalapeño, seeds removed, diced

½ cup sharp cheddar cheese or pepper Jack or vegan cheddar

1. Mix together the almond butter and sour cream.
2. For each quesadilla, spread the mixture on the bottom tortilla. Top with half the strawberries and jalapeños.
3. Sprinkle the cheddar on top.
4. Place the other tortilla on top of the cheese.
5. Place the quesadilla in a large skillet. Heat on medium and cook for 3–4 minutes, or until the bottom is golden brown. Carefully flip with a spatula and cook on the other side for 2 minutes.
6. Quarter the quesadilla. Repeat with the second quesadilla.

**MAKES
2 QUESADILLAS**

**PER SERVING
(1 QUESADILLA)**

Calories: 480

Calories from Fat: 189

Total Fat: 22.3g, 34%

Saturated Fat: 8.6g, 43%

Total Carb: 28.7g, 10%

Dietary Fiber: 4.3g, 17%

Sugars: 3.2g

Protein: 13.9g

Cholesterol: 35mg, 12%

Sodium: 203mg, 8%

Chocolate Almond Butter, page 23

Lacey Almond Crepes, page 30

Belgian Sweet Waffles, page 36

Banana Bread Oatmeal, page 39

*Vegan Almond Flour Muffins, page 55, **with Almond Flour Streusel Topping, page 56***

Almond Butter Muffins, page 62

Banana Almond Bread, page 65

Chocolate Almond Smoothie, page 83

Vanilla Almond Steamer, page 76

Double Dark Hot Cocoa, page 77

Almond Crunch Crackers with Sesame Seeds, page 90   *Almond Butter Hummus, page 92*

Creamy Almond Butter and Honey Apple Dip, page 93

Creamy Cauliflower Soup, page 130   *Creamy Tomato Soup with Grilled Cheese Croutons, page 127*

Almond Butter Browned Steak, page 154

Almond Butter Pesto, page 157

Almond Milk Alfredo, page 156

Korean Lettuce Wraps, page 172

Lazy Day Udon Noodles, page 156

Pumpkin Cookies, page 180

Flourless Chocolate Fudge Brownies, page 184,
with Coco-Coconut Buttercream Frosting, page 192

Pistachio Cherry Chocolate Biscotti, page 188

Primal Cookie Dough Power Bars, page 190   *Almond Flour Pie Crust, page 195*

Vanilla Almond Milk Custard Pie, page 196   *One-Bite Vanilla Almond Butter Cups, page 202*

Pear and Raspberry Almond Butter Sandwich

The combination of pears, raspberries, and almonds in this simple sandwich is inspired! Add a sprinkle of chia seeds, and enjoy a healthy little crunch, too! If you can't find raspberry honey, feel free to use any local honey for drizzling on top. Vegan eaters can swap in maple syrup instead.

D
gL
VE
VT

4 slices bread (gluten-free if desired)

2 tablespoons almond butter

1 ripe Bartlett or Bosc pear, cored and cut into ½-inch slices

¼ cup fresh raspberries

½ teaspoon chia seeds

2 teaspoons raspberry honey

1. Toast the bread.
2. For each sandwich, spread one-fourth of the almond butter on a slice of bread. Layer with half the pear slices, raspberries, and chia seeds. Drizzle with half the raspberry honey.
3. Spread the top slice with one-fourth of the almond butter and place on top.

**MAKES
2 SANDWICHES**

**PER SERVING
(1 SANDWICH)**

Calories: 369

Calories from Fat: 148

Total Fat: 11.7g, 18%

Saturated Fat: 1.2g, 6%

Total Carb: 27.4g, 9%

Dietary Fiber: 7.4g, 30%

Sugars: 14.9g

Protein: 5.6g

Cholesterol: 0mg, 0%

Sodium: 31mg, 1%

Raspberry Garden Grilled Sandwich

This combination of fruits and veggies may seem surprising, but it's really quite good. Though carrots and spinach are usually considered savory veggies, they are mild enough to work nicely with raspberries in this recipe. Try serving with a cold glass of almond milk for an afternoon nibble.

6 tablespoons chunky roasted almond butter

4 slices sourdough, gluten-free if desired

1 carrot, sliced into ribbons

1 cup baby spinach

½ cup fresh raspberries

2 tablespoons butter, softened, or Earth Balance

1. Spread 1 ½ tablespoons of almond butter on each of the four slices of bread.
2. Layer carrots, spinach and raspberries on top of two slices of the bread.
3. Place the second two slices almond-butter-side-down on top of the sandwich fillings.
4. Spread the top and bottom of the sandwiches with butter or Earth Balance spread.
5. Heat a grill pan or large skillet on the stove over medium heat. Grill the sandwiches on one side until light golden brown, about 2–3 minutes. Flip with a spatula and grill the other side until light golden brown, about 2 minutes more. Remove them from the pan, slice in half, and serve.

D · gl · VE · VT

**MAKES
2 SANDWICHES**

**PER SERVING
(1 SANDWICH)**

Calories: 395

Calories from Fat: 107

Total Fat: 35g, 54%

Saturated Fat: 9g, 45%

Total Carb: 15g, 5%

Dietary Fiber: 8g, 32%

Sugars: 5g

Protein: 10g

Cholesterol: 31mg, 10%

Sodium: 226mg, 9%

Thai-Style Almond Butter Sandwich

Almond butter turns into a savory, Thai-style addition in this bright sandwich with unexpected flavors. A fun way to enjoy a new, fresh combination of veggies, serve this dish for lunch or a light dinner.

D
gL
vE
vT

4 tablespoons almond butter

1 teaspoon lime juice

4 slices bread (gluten-free if desired)

2 slices red onion

8 thin slices of English or seedless cucumber

2 tablespoons shredded carrot

4 Thai or regular basil leaves, chopped

2 tablespoons bean sprouts

1. Cream the almond butter and lime juice together.
2. Toast the bread and spread half the almond butter mixture on two slices of bread. Divide the onion, cucumber, carrot, basil, and sprouts between the sandwiches.
3. Spread the remaining almond butter on the two remaining pieces of bread and place on top of the veggies. Slice and serve.

**MAKES
2 SANDWICHES**

**PER SERVING
(1 SANDWICH)**

Calories: 417

Calories from Fat: 208

Total Fat: 20.1g, 31%

Saturated Fat: 1.8g, 9%

Total Carb: 62.5g 21%

Dietary Fiber: 8.2g, 33%

Sugars: 2.0g

Protein: 16.8g

Cholesterol: 0mg, 0%

Sodium: 153mg, 6%

Thai-Style Grilled Cheese

Thai flavors pair flawlessly with almond butter, but chances are you haven't thought of putting them together with the classic goodness of grilled cheese! This recipe takes everything you know about a slab of cheese between two slices of bread and turns it into a gourmet taste experience.

(GF)
(GR)

**MAKES
4 SANDWICHES**

**PER SERVING
(1 SANDWICH)**

Calories: 235
Calories from Fat: 109
Total Fat: 12g, 18 %
Saturated Fat: 1g, 5 %
Total Carb: 27g, 9 %
Dietary Fiber: 2g, 8 %
Sugars: 5.0g
Protein: 6g, 12 %
Cholesterol: 0%
Sodium: 630mg, 26 %

FOR THE SPICY ALMOND SAUCE

1 tablespoon olive oil

2 scallions, finely chopped (Keep white and green parts separate.)

1 shallot, finely chopped

2 teaspoons grated ginger

3 tablespoons almond butter

2 tablespoons soy sauce

2 tablespoons apple cider vinegar

1 tablespoon raw honey, pure maple syrup, or brown sugar

1 teaspoon sesame oil

1 teaspoon dried hot red pepper flakes

FOR THE SANDWICH

4 tablespoons unsalted butter or Earth Balance, at room temperature

8 slices bread (gluten-free, if desired)

2 cups shredded sharp cheddar cheese

1 cup warm cooked chicken, shredded

1. To make the spicy almond sauce, heat the olive oil in a large skillet over medium–low heat until hot but not smoking. Add the whites of the scallions, the shallot, and ginger and cook for 1 minute.
2. Add ⅓ cup water and the almond butter, soy sauce, vinegar, honey, sesame oil, and pepper flakes. Cook for 5 minutes, stirring the sauce frequently until smooth.
3. For each sandwich, butter one side of each slice of bread.
4. Heat a small skillet over medium low heat. Place two slices of bread, butter side down in the pan.

5. Layer with ¼ cup of cheese, ¼ cup of chicken, scallion greens, and 2 tablespoons of the spicy almond sauce. Top with another ¼ cup of cheese and place another slice of bread on top, butter side up. Cook until golden brown, 3–4 minutes. Flip and cook for an additional 3 minutes. Repeat with the rest of the sandwiches.

6. Dip the sandwiches in the remaining spicy almond sauce.

Asian-Style Lettuce Wraps

Pretty little lettuce wraps are pulled together in minutes when you use rotisserie chicken. Once the meat is shredded, all you need is a bowl. No baking is required, so make this on a hot summer night when you simply don't feel like cooking. Paleo eaters can serve the filling in a lettuce wrap.

FOR THE CHICKEN SALAD

1 pound rotisserie chicken, shredded

2 cups broccoli or coleslaw

¼ cup diced scallions

1 tablespoon finely chopped ginger

1 tablespoon finely chopped garlic

1 teaspoon garlic gomasio (or toasted sesame seeds)

3 tablespoons lime juice

3 tablespoons avocado, grapeseed, or olive oil

FOR THE ALMOND BUTTER SAUCE

⅔ cup coconut milk

2 tablespoons almond butter

1 ½ tablespoons soy sauce, tamari, or Bragg Liquid Aminos

1 ½ tablespoons raw honey

8 leaves Bibb lettuce

1. In a large bowl, toss together all the chicken salad ingredients.
2. In a small bowl, whisk together the coconut milk, almond butter, soy sauce, and honey. Spoon the chicken mixture into the lettuce leaves. Drizzle with the almond butter sauce and serve.

MAKES 8 WRAPS

PER SERVING (1 WRAP)

Calories: 217

Calories from Fat: 125

Total Fat: 13.9g, 21%

Saturated Fat: 5.4g, 27%

Total Carb: 9.6g, 3%

Dietary Fiber: 1.5g, 6%

Sugars: 4.6g

Protein: 16.2g

Cholesterol: 41mg, 14%

Sodium: 386mg, 16%

Enlightened Monte Cristo

If you've never become acquainted with a Monte Cristo sandwich (basically a deep-fried ham and Swiss cheese sandwich), or even if you have, it's time to meet a healthier version. The original Monte Cristo calls for the sandwich to be battered and fried like a donut. This version is just as good, but better for you because it's grilled.

1 large egg

2 tablespoons almond milk

½ cup almond flour

4 slices ham

2 slices Swiss cheese

4 slices gluten-free bread

2 tablespoons butter or Earth Balance

1 tablespoon powdered sugar

4 tablespoons strawberry jam

1. Beat the egg and almond milk together in a small bowl.
2. Place the almond flour in a pie pan or other shallow dish.
3. For each sandwich, place one slice of ham and one slice of cheese between two slices of bread.
4. Heat the butter or Earth Balance in a large skillet over medium heat.
5. Dip the sandwiches one at a time into the egg mixture, then into the almond flour, making sure that each side is completely coated.
6. Place the sandwich in the skillet and cook for 3–4 minutes until golden brown. Turn the sandwich over and cook for an additional 3 minutes.
7. Sprinkle the sandwich with powdered sugar and dip it in strawberry jam.

**MAKES
2 SANDWICHES**

**PER SERVING
(1 SANDWICH)**

Calories: 279

Calories from Fat: 168

Total Fat: 37.7g, 58%

Saturated Fat: 18.1g, 91%

Total Carb: 83.4g, 28%

Dietary Fiber: 11.8g, 47%

Sugars: 7.2g

Protein: 28.0g

Cholesterol: 181mg, 60%

Sodium: 1086mg, 45%

Grilled Chicken Sandwich

Grilled chicken sandwiches are better than ever when paired with a sun-dried tomato and cilantro pesto. If you love cheese, a slice of provolone on top of each grilled chicken breast will make this dish even tastier.

GF
VE
VT

FOR THE ALMOND BUTTER AND SUN-DRIED TOMATO SPREAD

3 tablespoons almond butter

1 tablespoon finely diced oil-packed sun-dried tomatoes

1 tablespoon finely diced cilantro

FOR THE CHICKEN SANDWICH

2 chicken breasts or vegan chicken breasts

¼ cup olive oil

2 tablespoons lime juice

2 teaspoons chipotle chili powder

½ teaspoon kosher salt

Freshly ground pepper

4 sandwich rolls (gluten-free if desired)

4 lettuce leaves

8 slices tomatoes

4 slices onion

**MAKES
4 SANDWICHES**

**PER SERVING
(1 SANDWICH)**

Calories: 441

Calories from Fat: 238

Total Fat: 26.4g, 41%

Saturated Fat: 4.3g, 22%

Total Carb: 24.5g, 8%

Dietary Fiber: 1.5g, 6%

Sugars: 3.1g

Protein: 27.0g

Cholesterol: 62mg, 21%

Sodium: 575mg, 24%

1. To make the spread, cream the almond butter, sun-dried tomatoes, and cilantro together.
2. Pound the chicken breasts until they are 1 inch thick. Place in a resealable plastic bag with the oil, lime juice, chili powder, salt, and pepper to taste. Marinate for 1 hour.
3. Preheat a grill, grill pan, or griddle and grill the chicken breasts for 5–7 minutes on one side. Flip over and grill for another 5–7 minutes or until a meat thermometer inserted into the chicken registers at least 160°F. Cut each breast in half.
4. For each sandwich, spread the almond butter spread on one side of a halved roll. Layer the chicken, lettuce, tomato, and onion on the buttered side of the roll and cover with the top.

Spicy Brie Bagel

If you can find hot pepper or spicy blackberry jelly, this recipe will become a new favorite. Plain strawberry, raspberry, or blackberry jelly will work, too! Bagels are baked with almond butter, spicy jelly, and melted brie. Topped with peppery arugula, this sandwich is a simple way to go gourmet.

ⓖ ⓥⓣ

MAKES 4 SERVINGS

2 bagels, gluten-free if desired

4 tablespoons almond butter

4 tablespoons spicy jam or jelly

4 (1-ounce) slices brie

1 cup baby arugula

1 tablespoon avocado, grapeseed, or olive oil

¼ teaspoon sea salt

¼ teaspoon freshly ground pepper

1. Preheat the oven to 400°F.
2. Slice the bagels in half. Spread the almond butter and jam on the bagel. Top with the brie slices.
3. Place the bagels on a parchment-lined baking sheet. Bake for 7–10 minutes, or just until the brie begins to melt.
4. Remove from the oven and top the bagels with the arugula. Drizzle them with the avocado oil. Season with salt and pepper before serving.

**PER SERVING
(½ BAGEL)**

Servings: 4

Calories: 313

Calories from Fat: 121

Total Fat: 17g, 26%

Saturated Fat: 6g, 30%

Total Carb: 33g, 11%

Dietary Fiber: 3g, 12%

Sugars: 8g

Protein: 13g

Cholesterol: 28mg, 9%

Sodium: 574mg, 24%

Almond-Crusted Pesto Grilled Cheese Sandwich

Sometimes you want the usual, and sometimes you want the unique. This recipe gives you both. Almond flour lends a satisfying crunch to this pesto grilled cheese, adding a new depth and layer of flavor to a classic recipe.

4 slices bread (gluten-free, if desired)

3 tablespoons butter or Earth Balance

2 tablespoons almond flour

2 tablespoons Parmesan cheese

¼ cup pesto

4 tablespoons almond butter

2 tablespoons shredded Parmesan

2 red onion slices

2 tomato slices

4 slices mozzarella or vegan mozzarella

1. For each sandwich, spread two slices of the bread with a half-tablespoon of butter. In a shallow dish, use a fork to stir together the almond flour and Parmesan. Dip buttered side of the bread in the almond flour and Parmesan mixture.

2. Melt the remaining butter in a large nonstick skillet over medium-low heat. Drop the bread slices coated-side down into the pan.

3. Divide the pesto and Parmesan in half, spreading it on top of the bread slices as they brown on the grill pan. Top each with half the red onion, tomatoes, and mozzarella.

4. Spread the almond butter on the remaining two slices of bread, and place them butter-side-up on the mozzarella. Flip the sandwiches once they are golden brown, about 2–4 minutes, and cook for an additional 2–4 minutes, or until golden brown on the second side.

gf

MAKES 2 SANDWICHES

PER SERVING (1 SANDWICH)

Calories: 576

Calories from Fat: 331

Total Fat: 54.1g, 83%

Saturated Fat: 18.8g, 94%

Total Carb: 9.1g, 3%

Dietary Fiber: 2.0g, 8%

Sugars: 2.8g

Protein: 10.2g

Cholesterol: 69mg, 23%

Sodium: 354mg, 15%

Almond Butter Chicken Salad

Chicken salad gets a protein (and flavor) kick when almond butter is added to the sauce. This recipe calls for mayonnaise or vegan mayonnaise, but paleo eaters can replace the mayonnaise with ¼ cup coconut cream—the thick white layer found at the top in cans of full-fat coconut milk. To easily separate coconut cream from coconut milk, place the can of coconut milk in the fridge overnight. The solids will stick together and separate from the milk, making it easy to scoop out of the can, and right into your chicken salad.

D
GL
VE
VT

MAKES 8 SERVINGS

**PER SERVING
(1 SANDWICH)**

Calories: 309

Calories from Fat: 39

Total Fat: 25g, 38%

Saturated Fat: 3g,
  15%

Total Carb: 9g, 3%

Dietary Fiber: 3g, 12%

Sugars: 5g

Protein: 14g

Cholesterol: 22mg, 7%

Sodium: 361mg, 15%

¼ cup creamy almond butter

¼ cup mayonnaise or vegan mayo

1 tablespoon honey

Juice of 1 lemon

2 cups cooked, shredded chicken or vegan chicken shreds

½ cup halved red grapes

¼ cup chopped scallions

3 tablespoons chopped pecans

¾ teaspoon sea salt

½ teaspoon freshly ground pepper

8 small croissants or dinner rolls, gluten-free if desired

1. In a large bowl, whisk together the almond butter, mayo, honey, and lemon juice. Stir in the chicken, grapes, scallions, and pecans. Sprinkle with salt and pepper.

2. Spoon the mixture on the croissants and enjoy immediately or store it in the fridge in an airtight container for up to two days.

8

Soups

Soups are some of the easiest meals to make and offer a simple approach to filling your kitchen table with vegetables in a family-friendly way. Even picky eaters will try unfamiliar ingredients when they are simmered into a soup. In this chapter, I've made some of the soups you already adore into healthy recipes, and others might be new to your tasting experience. Try all of them! With fresh, easy-to-find ingredients and incredible flavors, these soups showcase the versatility and beauty of almond butters and almond milks in a way you may not have appreciated until now.

Spicy Carrot Soup

The natural sweetness of carrots is so nice when combined with the zing of lime and a little spicy heat. This flavorful soup is warm and bright. Heat it up on autumn evenings or serve it chilled in the summer. Pair it with **MILE-HIGH BISCUITS (PAGE 53)** *or add a dollop of yogurt for a gourmet garnish.*

2 tablespoons avocado, grapeseed, or olive oil

½ onion, finely chopped

1 clove garlic, finely chopped

1 pound baby carrots, peeled

4 cups vegetable stock

2 tablespoons creamy roasted almond butter

1 tablespoon tamari, soy sauce, or Bragg Liquid Aminos

1 tablespoon Sriracha

Juice and zest of 1 lime

½ teaspoon salt

½ teaspoon freshly ground pepper

1 tablespoon toasted sesame oil (optional)

½ teaspoon red pepper flakes (optional)

¼ cup fresh cilantro, chopped

1. In a large pot, heat the oil over medium-high heat.
2. Add the onions and garlic and sauté until softened. Add the carrots and stock. Cover, bring to a boil, and cook until the carrots are tender, about 20 minutes.
3. Transfer the mixture to a high-speed blender or use a hand blender to puree. Stir in the almond butter, tamari, Sriracha, lime juice, lime zest, salt and pepper.
4. Sprinkle the soup with salt right before serving. Serve it immediately with a drizzle of sesame oil (if using) and a sprinkling of red pepper flakes (if using) and cilantro.

MAKES 4 SERVINGS

PER SERVING (¼ RECIPE)

Calories: 311

Calories from Fat: 134

Total Fat: 14g, 22%

Saturated Fat: 2g, 10%

Total Carb: 41g, 14%

Dietary Fiber: 8g, 32%

Sugars: 10g

Protein: 9g

Cholesterol: 2mg, 1%

Sodium: 1756mg, 73%

Creamy Tomato Soup
with Grilled Cheese Croutons

Homemade tomato soup is the easiest dinner ever. Grilled cheese croutons that you also make yourself lend a trendy, fun flair to the soup. If you're avoiding dairy and carbs, try garnishing this dish with a sprinkle of freshly chopped basil.

D **GL** **GR** **PL** **VE** **VT**

MAKES 4 SERVINGS

FOR THE SOUP

1 tablespoon olive oil

½ small sweet onion, finely diced

1 (28-ounce) can diced tomatoes or fire-roasted diced tomatoes

2 cups unsweetened almond milk

1 teaspoons honey or maple syrup

1 teaspoon salt

FOR THE GRILLED CHEESE CROUTONS

4 slices thick-cut white bread (like Texas Toast) or gluten-free bread

½ cup sliced sharp cheddar (or vegan cheddar melts)

Nonstick olive oil cooking spray

1. Heat the olive oil in a large pot over medium-high heat. Add the onions and cook until softened, 2–3 minutes. Add the tomatoes, almond milk, maple syrup, and salt. Heat the soup just until boiling. Cover and remove from heat.
2. To prepare the croutons, heat a grill pan or large skillet over medium heat.
3. Layer the cheese between two slices of bread. Spray the top and bottom of sandwich with nonstick olive oil cooking spray.
4. Place on a hot grill pan and cook until golden brown on both sides. Remove it and cool slightly before slicing into 1-inch cubes with a sharp, serrated knife. Repeat this process with the remaining bread and cheese for the second batch of croutons.
5. Serve the croutons on top of the tomato soup.

Note: For paleo eaters, serve this soup without the croutons and top with coconut-milk yogurt and roasted pumpkin seeds (pepitas).

PER SERVING (¼ RECIPE)

Calories: 226

Calories from Fat: 97

Total Fat: 10.8g, 17%

Saturated Fat: 3.7g, 19%

Total Carb: 25.8g, 9%

Dietary Fiber: 3.8g, 15%

Sugars: 8.3g

Protein: 8.2g

Cholesterol: 15mg, 5%

Sodium: 973mg, 41%

Sweet Corn Soup
with Herbed Tomato Salsa

This recipe is splendid served on a summer day with fresh corn, but don't let that keep you from making a batch of this enjoyable soup any time of the year with frozen sweet corn. Serve with a leafy, green salad and loaf of crusty bread for a simple, delicious, healthy meal.

D
GL
GR
VE
VT

FOR THE SOUP

½ tablespoon butter or olive oil

½ sweet onion, finely diced

Kernels cut from 6 ears of corn or 2 cups frozen sweet corn

2 cups vegetable broth

2 cups almond milk

½ teaspoon salt

3 tablespoons sugar or raw honey

FOR THE HERBED TOMATO SALSA

2 heirloom tomatoes, diced

¼ cup chopped fresh basil

2 tablespoons chopped fresh marjoram, sage, and/or thyme

½ tablespoon malt vinegar

1 tablespoon olive oil

Juice of ½ lemon

MAKES 6 SERVINGS

**PER SERVING
(¼ RECIPE)**

Calories: 212

Calories from Fat: 209

Total Fat: 6g, 9%

Saturated Fat: 3g, 15%

Total Carb: 36g, 12%

Dietary Fiber: 3g, 12%

Sugars: 17g

Protein: 8g

Cholesterol: 12mg, 4%

Sodium: 659mg, 27%

1. Heat the butter in a large pot over medium heat. Add the onions and cook until softened, about 2–3 minutes. Add the corn and cook for 2 minutes. Add the vegetable broth, almond milk, salt, and sugar.

2. Remove from heat. Transfer it to a blender and puree in batches until it's smooth. Return the pureed soup to the pot and heat to just before boiling. If you want the corn to be less like chowder and more like soup, add an additional ½–1 cup

of almond milk or broth to thin it. (I like it thin, so always add that extra bit of liquid.)

3. For the salsa, mix all the ingredients together in a medium bowl.

4. Spoon the salsa into the center of each hot bowl of corn soup. Serve immediately.

Creamy Cauliflower Soup

Whether you need an elegant soup for a party or a quick weeknight dinner for your family, this soup delivers. The creaminess is unmatched, the health factor is substantial for every type of diet, and it's easy to prepare. Try it and decide for yourself. (Fair warning: chances are, you're going to fall in love!)

1 large head cauliflower, which has been boiled until very tender

2–3 cups almond milk

2 cloves roasted garlic

½ teaspoon cardamom

Salt

1 cup halved red grapes

½ cup sliced almonds

½ cup chopped scallions

1. Place the cauliflower in an industrial-strength blender. A regular or hand blender will work, as well, but the final consistency may be slightly chunkier. Add 2 cups of the almond milk, the roasted garlic, and the cardamom to the blender. Blend until smooth and creamy. Add more almond milk, if a thinner texture is preferred.

2. Cover and blend until hot, or transfer it to a large pot on medium-high heat, and cook until steaming but not boiling.

3. Serve the soup topped with the grapes, almonds, and scallions.

MAKES 4 SERVINGS

**PER SERVING
(¼ RECIPE)**

Calories: 188

Calories from Fat: 90

Total Fat: 10g, 15%

Saturated Fat: 3g, 15%

Total Carb: 18g, 6%

Dietary Fiber: 3g, 12%

Sugars: 13g

Protein: 10g

Cholesterol: 14mg, 5%

Sodium: 592 mg, 25%

Butternut Squash Soup with Almond Yogurt Swirl

This soup is simple and perfect—a great starter soup for dinner parties or a great quick dinner for chilly autumn nights. To pull this recipe together quicker than ever, look for cubed frozen butternut squash in the freezer section of health food stores. They nix all the prep work normally required for peeling and cubing the squash and make it easy to make a batch of soup in minutes.

(gL) (gR) (pL) (vE) (vT)

1 tablespoon olive oil

2 shallots, diced

1 small butternut squash, peeled and cubed

1 cup vegetable broth

2 cups unsweetened almond milk

3 tablespoons almond butter

Pinch of nutmeg

Salt and freshly ground pepper

1 cup vanilla almond milk yogurt

2 tablespoons chopped fresh basil

1. Heat the olive oil in a large pot over medium-high heat. Add the shallots and squash and cook until the shallots are softened (about 2 minutes). Add the vegetable broth, cover, and cook until the squash is very soft, about 15–20 minutes. Add the almond milk, almond butter, and nutmeg. Season to taste with salt and pepper.
2. Transfer the soup to a blender and puree in batches until smooth.
3. Return the pureed soup to the pot and heat until it's hot. Swirl in a tablespoon of yogurt. Garnish with chopped basil.

MAKES 6 SERVINGS

PER SERVING (⅙ RECIPE)

Calories: 131

Calories from Fat: 107

Total Fat: 11.9g, 18%

Saturated Fat: 1.2g, 6%

Total Carb: 2.9g, 1%

Dietary Fiber: 1.0g, 4%

Protein: 4.3g

Cholesterol: 0mg, 0%

Sodium: 320mg, 13%

Loaded Baked Sweet Potato Soup

Loaded Baked Sweet Potato Soup is a fun, healthier twist on the classic. Just toss sweet potatoes in the oven until tender whenever you have an hour or two, then store them in the fridge (for up to a week) until you're ready to prep and serve this delicious meal. Top with any of your favorite toppings. Suggestions are given below, but your imagination is the only limit!

3 tablespoons coconut oil

1 sweet onion, chopped

4 cloves garlic

4 large baked sweet potatoes, peeled and diced

2 cups unsweetened almond milk

2 cups vegetable broth

Salt

TOPPING OPTIONS

crumbled bacon, plain Greek yogurt, diced scallions, shredded cheddar cheese, chopped walnuts, garlicky wilted spinach, crumbled feta cheese, diced sun-dried tomatoes

1. Melt the coconut oil in a large pot over medium-high heat. Add the onion and garlic and cook for 1–2 minutes, or until softened. Add the diced sweet potatoes, almond milk, and vegetable broth.

2. Transfer to a blender and puree in batches until smooth. Return the pureed soup to the pot and heat until it's hot. Season to taste with salt.

3. Spoon the soup into bowls and top with your favorite items from the list above.

D **gL** **gR** **pL** **VE** **VT**

MAKES 6–8 SERVINGS

PER SERVING (⅙ RECIPE, BEFORE TOPPINGS)

Calories: 200

Calories from Fat: 75

Total Fat: 8.3g, 13%

Saturated Fat: 6.0g, 30%

Total Carb: 27.8g, 9%

Dietary Fiber: 4.7g, 19%

Sugars: 8.8g

Protein: 4.7g

Cholesterol: 0mg, 0%

Sodium: 385mg, 16%

Enlightened Clam Chowder

Clam chowder is traditionally a decadent indulgence, but it doesn't have to be that way! This incredibly delicious, lightened-up dish is so good, no one will guess it's not the full-fat version.

2 tablespoons olive oil

1 large yellow onion, diced

4 cloves garlic, minced

2 stalks celery, diced

½ cup white wine

1 pound red potatoes, diced

2 cups low-sodium chicken or veggie broth

3 (6.5-ounce) cans clams, drained, liquid reserved

1 teaspoon celery salt

3 cups almond milk

¼ cup cornstarch

Salt and freshly ground pepper

¼ cup chopped fresh parsley

MAKES 6 SERVINGS

**PER SERVING
(⅙ RECIPE)**

Calories: 398

Calories from Fat: 200

Total Fat: 9g, 14%

Saturated Fat: 2g, 10%

Total Carb: 29g, 10%

Dietary Fiber: 2g, 8%

Sugars: 8g

Protein: 20g

Cholesterol: 46mg, 15%

Sodium: 881mg, 37%

1. Heat the olive oil in a medium pot over medium-high heat. Add the diced onion, garlic, and celery and cook until softened, 1–2 minutes. Add the wine and bring to a boil, then toss in the potatoes, chicken broth, and reserved clam juice. Add the celery salt, then just enough water to cover the potatoes. Cover and bring to a boil until the potatoes are easily pierced with a fork, about 10 to 12 minutes.

2. In a large pot, whisk together the almond milk and cornstarch. Place the pot on medium heat and cook until the almond milk thickens, about 3–4 minutes.

3. Pour the potato mixture into the almond milk, add the clams, and stir. Season to taste with salt and pepper. Garnish the chowder with fresh parsley before serving.

Thai Curry Chicken Noodle Soup

Everyone loves chicken noodle soup. And sometimes, classics aren't made to be messed with. But turn the traditional into Thai, and you'll have a new favorite recipe in your house! Though the list of ingredients for this recipe might seem daunting, it's worth the hunt around the grocery store, since almost everything is available between the produce section and the Asian/Indian foods aisle. Turn the recipe vegan/vegetarian easily by replacing the chicken stock with vegetable stock and the chicken with chopped vegan chicken strips, or go paleo by replacing the rice noodles with bean sprouts. Can't find garam masala? Chole masala powder is available at major retailers and works just as well. Or, swap in curry powder and a pinch of cardamom instead.

2 tablespoons coconut oil

1 shallot, diced

3 cloves garlic, minced

2 Thai green chilies, minced

1 tablespoon red curry paste

1 tablespoon mild yellow curry powder

1 teaspoon garam masala or chole masala powder

1 pound cooked chicken breasts or vegan chicken strips, diced

1 red bell pepper, sliced thin

2 cups snow peas

4 cups chicken stock or vegetable stock

1 (14.5-ounce) can coconut milk

2 cups unsweetened almond milk

Juice of 2 limes

2 ounces rice noodles or 2 cups bean sprouts

3 cups spinach

½ cup julienned scallions

½ cup chopped cilantro

½ cup sliced almonds

MAKES 6 SERVINGS

PER SERVING
(⅙ RECIPE)

Calories: 313

Calories from Fat: 250

Total Fat: 14g, 22%

Saturated Fat: 7g, 35%

Total Carb: 21g, 7%

Dietary Fiber: 3g, 12%

Sugars: 6g

Protein: 27g

Cholesterol: 53mg, 18%

Sodium: 581mg, 24%

1. Melt the coconut oil in a large pot over medium heat. Add the shallot, garlic, and green chilies and cook until softened, 1–2 minutes. Add the red curry paste, curry powder, and garam masala, stirring for about 1 minute or just until the spices become aromatic. Immediately add the boiled chicken, red bell pepper, and snow peas. Pour in the chicken stock, coconut milk, almond milk, and lime juice. Add the rice noodles. Bring the soup to a boil, and cook just until the noodles are softened, 6–8 minutes.
2. Remove from the heat and stir in the spinach. Serve steaming bowls of soup topped with the scallions, cilantro, and almonds.

Velvet Almond Soup

This creamy soup will surprise you with its simplicity. After sautéing some onion and leeks, just toss all the ingredients into a large pot, boil, then puree in your blender for a truly comforting soup. Paleo eaters can swap a sweet potato or steamed cauliflower for the potato. If you like baked potato soup, this recipe works well as a base for all of your favorite baked potato toppings, too. Try serving a bowl with a variety of à la carte toppings like grated cheese, bacon bits, and/or scallions for a fun twist.

GL **GR** **PL** **VE** **VT**

MAKES 4 SERVINGS

PER SERVING (¼ RECIPE)

Calories: 327

Calories from Fat: 211

Total Fat: 12g, 18%

Saturated Fat: 2g, 10%

Total Carb: 47g, 16%

Dietary Fiber: 5g, 20%

Sugars: 9g

Protein: 11g

Cholesterol: 6mg, 2%

Sodium: 629mg, 26%

1 tablespoon olive oil

½ yellow onion, diced

2 leeks, white portions only, sliced thin

1 large russet potato, peeled and diced (paleo eaters, see recipe headnote)

3 cups vegetable broth

1 cup almond milk

2 tablespoons almond butter

½ teaspoon ground ginger

¼ teaspoon nutmeg powder

Salt

1 tablespoon fresh rosemary needles

1. Heat the olive oil in a medium pot over medium-high heat. Add the onion and leeks and cook until softened, 1–2 minutes. Add the diced potato and vegetable broth, cover, and bring to a boil. Cook the potato until softened, about 9 to 10 minutes.
2. Remove from the heat. Add the almond milk, almond butter, ginger, and nutmeg.
3. Transfer the soup to a blender and puree in batches until smooth.
4. Return the pureed soup to the pot, heat until hot, and season to taste with salt.
5. Serve steaming in bowls topped with the rosemary.

Almond Chicken Soup

Perfect for a quick weeknight meal, this soup is familiar-tasting enough to be family-friendly but introduces new flavors to your kitchen table. Sweet potatoes, bok choy, and almond butter help create a homey dish that everyone will ask for again and again. Vegan and vegetarian eaters can make this soup with diced vegan chicken strips or without any chicken at all! The sweet potato and bok choy keep the broth hearty and filling, even in the absence of meat.

D
DL
VE
VT

MAKES 4 SERVINGS

PER SERVING (¼ RECIPE)

Calories: 451

Calories from Fat: 217

Total Fat: 21g, 32%

Saturated Fat: 2g, 10%

Total Carb: 18g, 6%

Dietary Fiber: 6g, 24%

Sugars: 4g

Protein: 49g

Cholesterol: 126mg, 42%

Sodium: 816mg, 34%

4 cups chicken or vegetable stock

½ sweet onion, diced

2 garlic cloves, minced

1 large sweet potato, peeled and diced

8 ounces boneless, skinless chicken breast or vegan chicken strips, cut into 1-inch cubes

2 cups coarsely chopped bok choy

½ cup almond butter

2 tablespoons minced fresh ginger

Juice of 1 lime

Salt

Freshly ground pepper

2 tablespoons chopped fresh mint

1. Place the chicken stock, onion, garlic, sweet potato, chicken, and bok choy in a large pot on medium-high heat. Cover, bring to a boil, then reduce the heat to a simmer for 20 minutes, or until the chicken is cooked through and the sweet potato is softened.
2. Transfer 1 cup of the soup broth to a small bowl. Whisk in the almond butter, ginger, and lime juice.
3. Stir this mixture into the soup, and heat until the soup is piping hot.
4. Season to taste with salt and pepper. Serve immediately, garnished with the mint.

Chilled Strawberry Almond Soup

No cooking required! This light soup is the right complement to a summer day. Just whir everything together in a blender and serve it up quickly. It's beautiful when garnished with fresh strawberry slices and fresh mint. Paleo eaters will want to omit the almond liqueur.

4 cups fresh or frozen strawberries, cleaned and hulled

¼ cup vanilla almond milk

2 tablespoons almond butter

2 tablespoons almond liqueur (like Disaronno)

1 teaspoon finely chopped fresh jalapeño

1 tablespoon chopped fresh mint

1. Place the strawberries, almond milk, almond butter, almond liqueur, and jalapeño in a blender. Puree until smooth.
2. Pour it into bowls, garnish with mint, and serve immediately.

(D) (gL) (gR) (pL) (vE) (vT)

MAKES 4 SERVINGS

PER SERVING (¼ RECIPE)

Calories: 141

Calories from Fat: 41

Total Fat: 4.5g, 7%

Saturated Fat: 0g

Total Carb: 14.6g, 5%

Dietary Fiber: 3.4g, 14%

Sugars: 8.9g

Protein: 1.8g

Cholesterol: 0mg, 0%

Sodium: 0mg, 0%

9

Dinner

Though it may feel like you've been stuck in a dinner rut for the last decade, the way we enjoy our evening meals has changed dramatically over the years. Once a space for the staples of meat and potatoes, the addition of global produce and products to local grocery store shelves has meant hundreds of new options.

Chances are, however, you're still relying on familiar comfort food, serving up spaghetti or making tacos once a week.

This chapter is a happy compilation of favorite recipes with new ingredients. Here are mealtime combinations that will get you out of your dinnertime rut and bring new flavors to your kitchen table, while still offering some tried-and-true classics made better or more flavorful with the addition of almond products.

From quick and simple weeknight dishes to slow-cooked weekend feasts, this chapter is dedicated to expanding your options, while also offering easy, delicious meals made with the goodness of almonds.

Grok's Chicken Fingers

Who needs fast-food chicken tenders? A batch of home-baked, crispy-tender chicken strips can be yours in no time at all with this easy, paleo-friendly, gluten-free recipe. Dip in raw honey and serve with the **MILE-HIGH BISCUITS (PAGE 53)** *for a dinner reminiscent of classic southern comfort food.*

1 pound boneless skinless chicken breasts
½ cup almond milk
1 egg
1 cup blanched almond flour
1 tablespoon paprika
1 teaspoon onion powder
1 teaspoon garlic powder
½ teaspoon sea salt
½ teaspoon freshly ground pepper

1. Preheat the oven to 350°F.
2. Cut the chicken into 1-inch-thick strips.
3. In a shallow bowl, whisk together the egg and almond milk. Place the chicken strips in the egg mixture and turn to coat both sides of the chicken.
4. In a large, zip-top bag, combine the almond flour, paprika, onion powder, garlic powder, salt, and pepper. Shake to mix, then place several chicken strips in the almond flour mixture and shake the bag to coat the chicken.
5. Transfer the coated chicken strips to a parchment-lined baking sheet. Bake in the preheated oven for 14–19 minutes, or until the chicken fingers are cooked through. Cool slightly before serving.

MAKES 4 SERVINGS

PER SERVING (¼ RECIPE)

Calories: 284
Calories from Fat: 142
Total Fat: 5g, 8%
Saturated Fat: 1g 5%
Total Carb: 28g, 9%
Dietary Fiber: 2g, 8%
Sugars: 2g
Protein: 30g
Cholesterol: 116mg, 39%
Sodium: 457mg, 19%

My Favorite Fried Chicken

Sometimes you just want comfort food. But comfort food can be such a diet buzzkill, especially when you're trying to avoid gluten. This recipe delivers a crunchy, gluten-free fried chicken that is as easy and delicious as the original. The secret is the coconut oil, though if you don't have it in the house you can also use avocado oil. Served with **ALMOND FLOUR POLENTA (PAGE 103)** or **MASHED CAULIFLOWER (PAGE 101)** and **CREAMY PEPPER GRAVY (102)**, you won't feel like you're giving up anything at all, even though all the gluten is missing!

2 cups coconut oil for frying

1 ½ cups unsweetened almond milk

1 tablespoon white vinegar

1 whole chicken, skin-on, cut-up

1 ½ cups blanched almond flour

¾ teaspoon sea salt

½ teaspoon cayenne

1 teaspoon dried thyme

1. Preheat the oven to 350°F.
2. Heat the coconut oil in a large skillet over medium-high heat.
3. In a shallow bowl, whisk together the almond milk and vinegar. Press the chicken in the milk mixture, rolling it around to coat.
4. In a second shallow dish, stir together the almond flour, salt, cayenne, and thyme. Dip chicken in the almond flour mixture, then transfer it to the skillet and fry it in the hot oil until golden brown, about 2–3 minutes on one side, and 1–2 minutes on the second side.
5. Once the chicken is browned on all sides, transfer to a parchment-lined baking sheet and bake for 12–15 minutes more, until the chicken is cooked through. Serve with your favorite fried chicken sides.

MAKES 8 SERVINGS

PER SERVING (⅛ RECIPE)

Calories: 449

Calories from Fat: 353

Total Fat: 22g, 34%

Saturated Fat: 14g, 70%

Total Carb: 20g, 7%

Dietary Fiber: 1g, 4%

Sugars: 2g

Protein: 41g

Cholesterol: 145mg, 48%

Sodium: 440mg, 18%

Crispy Chick'n Almond Nuggets

Meatless substitutes can put a dent in your budget and are often full of preservatives and other ingredients you can't even pronounce. But these homemade nuggets made of plain, natural ingredients are fully vegan and packed full of protein, thanks to almond flour and garbanzo beans. Easy to make, easier to eat. Try dipping these nuggets in vegan barbecue sauce, vegan ranch dressing, or fresh jam. They're also great served on top of greens with sliced tomatoes and Italian dressing.

1 cup blanched almond flour

1 teaspoon onion powder

1 teaspoon garlic powder

1 teaspoon salt

½ teaspoon freshly ground pepper

1 tablespoon olive oil

1 cup garbanzo beans, drained

1 clove garlic

2 tablespoons chopped onions

½ of 1 (14-ounce) block firm tofu

2 tablespoons nutritional yeast

2 tablespoons flaxseed meal

1 tablespoon tamari, soy sauce, or Bragg Liquid Aminos

Nonstick olive oil spray

1. Preheat the oven to 350°F.
2. In a large bowl, stir together the almond flour, onion powder, garlic powder, salt, and pepper. Remove ½ cup of the mixture and set it aside.
3. In a food processor, pulse the olive oil, garbanzo beans, garlic, onions, and tofu until very smooth. Add the garbanzo bean mixture to the bowl with the almond flour. Stir in the nutritional yeast, flaxseed meal, and tamari.
4. Make each "nugget" by pressing 2 tablespoons of the mixture into a nugget shape. Dredge the nuggets in the remaining

GL

GR

VE

VT

MAKES 4 SERVINGS

PER SERVING (¼ RECIPE)

Calories: 352

Calories from Fat: 191

Total Fat: 12g, 18%

Saturated Fat: 2g, 10%

Total Carb: 45g, 15%

Dietary Fiber: 7g, 28%

Sugars: 0g

Protein: 18g

Cholesterol: 0mg, 0%

Sodium: 984mg, 41%

almond flour mixture. Place them on a parchment-lined baking sheet and spray generously with the oil spray.

5. Bake for 15 minutes, then turn over the nuggets, spray again with the oil spray, and return them to the oven for another 15 minutes or until golden brown. Serve immediately.

Almond-Chicken Satay

Fans of Thai take-out will go wild over this simple almond chicken satay. Grab some skewers and serve batches of this as a high-protein entrée or as an appetizer for dinner parties.

FOR THE MARINADE

1 cup unsweetened almond milk

½ cup roughly chopped cilantro

2 scallions, chopped

1 ½ tablespoons soy sauce, tamari, or Bragg Liquid Aminos

2 tablespoons grated ginger

2 tablespoons lime juice

1 teaspoon cumin

½ teaspoon kosher salt

1 pound boneless, skinless chicken tenders or vegan chicken strips

FOR THE SAUCE

1 ½ cups almond milk

½ cup almond butter

¾ cup chicken stock

2 scallions (white and green parts), diced

2 tablespoons lime juice

1 ½ teaspoons cayenne

½ teaspoon kosher salt

Special Equipment: Bamboo skewers, soaked in cold water

1. Put the marinade ingredients into a large zip-top plastic bag. Add the chicken and marinate in the refrigerator for 3 hours.
2. Remove the chicken from the marinade and thread onto the skewers. Discard the marinade.
3. Preheat a grill or grill pan to medium heat and cook the chicken for 5–8 minutes, turning once.

MAKES 4 SERVINGS

PER SERVING (¼ RECIPE)

Calories: 389

Calories from Fat: 238

Total Fat: 26.5g, 41%

Saturated Fat: 7.0g, 35%

Total Carb: 12.4g, 4%

Dietary Fiber: 6.0g, 24%

Sugars: 2.0g

Protein: 34.5g

Cholesterol: 210mg, 70%

Sodium: 1209mg, 50%

4. While the chicken is grilling start the sauce. Whisk the almond milk, almond butter, and chicken stock together in a medium saucepan over medium heat. Once the sauce has reached a uniform consistency (about 3–5 minutes), add the scallions, lime juice, cayenne, and salt. Remove from the heat.
5. Serve the chicken with the satay sauce.

Spanish Almond Chicken

Truly good Spanish food has layers of flavor. This recipe is simple to make, but full of flavor complexities—ideal for cold winter nights when you want something warm and comforting yet vibrant. Served over long-grain rice, this dish is a true star. Paleo eaters will want to avoid the sherry when cooking the sauce, and can serve this alongside mashed cauliflower or sautéed zucchini.

½ cup sliced almonds

3 tablespoons butter or avocado or grapeseed oil

6 boneless skinless chicken breasts

1 clove garlic, finely chopped

1 ½ cups chicken stock or sherry

2 oranges, juiced and zested

1 tablespoon tomato paste

1 tablespoon creamy almond butter

3 tablespoons golden raisins

½ cup sliced green olives

1. Preheat the oven to 350°F.
2. Heat a large nonstick skillet over medium-high heat. Add the almonds to the skillet and stir with a wooden spoon until golden brown and toasted. Transfer them to a small dish and set aside.
3. Drizzle the skillet with 1 tablespoon of the butter. Brown the chicken breasts on both sides and transfer to a 9 × 13-inch baking dish.
4. Add the remaining butter to the skillet. When melted, toss the garlic into the butter and cook for 1 minute, until aromatic. Add the chicken stock and cook until reduced, then whisk the orange juice and zest, tomato paste, and almond butter into the skillet. Add the raisins, olives, and the toasted almonds to the sauce.
5. Pour the sauce over the chicken breasts. Bake for 18–22 minutes, or just until the chicken breasts are cooked through. Serve the chicken covered in sauce.

D
gf
gR
pl

MAKES 6 SERVINGS

PER SERVING
(⅙ RECIPE)

Calories: 399

Calories from Fat: 83

Total Fat: 24g, 37%

Saturated Fat: 6g, 30%

Total Carb: 16g, 5%

Dietary Fiber: 5g, 20%

Sugars: 6g

Protein: 33g

Cholesterol: 91mg, 30%

Sodium: 565mg, 24%

Almond Butter Veggie Burgers

This recipe may just be better than meat-based burgers. Made with grated sweet potatoes, almond butter, and almond flour, it's full of protein and even more full of flavor. Because the burgers bake in the oven, they're easy to stir together and cook while you clean up the kitchen and prep the rest of dinner. Healthy, quick, and simple, these may be the best veggie burgers ever!

(D)
(gL)
(gR)
(pL)
(vE)
(vT)

MAKES 6 SERVINGS

3 cups grated sweet potatoes
½ cup almond butter
½ cup almond flour
¼ cup very finely chopped onions
4 tablespoons tomato paste
½ teaspoon salt
½ tablespoon onion powder

**PER SERVING
(1 BURGER)**

Calories: 225
Calories from Fat: 118
Total Fat: 11g, 17%
Saturated Fat: 1g, 5%
Total Carb: 28g, 9%
Dietary Fiber: 5g, 20%
Sugars: 5g
Protein: 7g
Cholesterol: 0mg, 0%
Sodium: 358mg, 15%

1. Preheat the oven to 350°F.
2. In a large bowl, mix together all the ingredients. Stir together until well mixed.
3. Form the mixture into six firmly compacted patties and place the on a baking sheet lined with parchment paper.
4. Bake for 35 minutes, then use a spatula to flip the patties and cook on the second side for an additional 15 minutes. Remove and serve as you would hamburgers.

Variations

Vegan Burgers. Serve these scrumptious burgers on hamburger buns with vegan mayo, avocado, and sprouts.

Paleo Burgers. Serve these burgers sans buns, with slices of avocado on top and a drizzle of avocado oil, salt, and pepper.

Gluten-Free Burgers. Don't have gluten-free burger buns? No problem. These burgers taste great when served open-faced on a slice of toasted gluten-free bread or sourdough.

Perfect Eggplant Parmigia-no

Eggplant can be a turn-off for lots of eaters, mostly because if it's not cooked right, it's just not that fun to eat. But this recipe cooks it right. Better yet, it cooks it gluten-free, vegan, and paleo-friendly. So, it's the sort of dish that everyone can sit down to and enjoy. Serve with **ALMOND FLOUR POLENTA (PAGE 103)** *and your favorite marinara sauce for a quick, simple dinner.*

½ cup avocado oil or coconut oil for frying

½ cup almond milk

1 ½ tablespoons coconut oil

1 tablespoon white vinegar

¾ teaspoon sea salt

1 cup almond flour

½ tablespoon Italian seasoning

1 teaspoon garlic powder

½ teaspoon smoked paprika

1 large eggplant, sliced into ¼-inch pieces

½ cup marinara or spaghetti sauce

½ cup grated mozzarella or vegan mozzarella (optional)

1 tablespoon chopped fresh basil

1. Preheat the oven to 400°F. Heat the frying oil in a large skillet over medium heat.
2. Place the almond milk and coconut oil in a small, microwave-safe dish. Microwave just until the coconut oil is melted, about 90 seconds. Whisk in the vinegar and ¼ teaspoon of the salt.
3. In a small bowl, mix together the flour, Italian seasoning, garlic powder, paprika, and remaining ½ teaspoon of salt.
4. .Dip the eggplant slices in the almond milk mixture, then in the almond flour mixture.
5. Fry the eggplant slices on one side until golden brown, about 45–60 seconds. Flip and fry them on the second side until golden brown, about 30–60 seconds.

MAKES 4 SERVINGS

**PER SERVING
(¼ RECIPE)**

Calories: 262

Calories from Fat: 199

Total Fat: 22.1g, 34%

Saturated Fat: 13.3g, 66%

Total Carb: 12.7g, 4%

Dietary Fiber: 6.7g, 27%

Sugars: 4.5g

Protein: 7.5g

Cholesterol: 9mg, 3%

Sodium: 438mg, 18%

6. Layer the fried eggplant in a 9 × 9-inch baking dish as needed to make it all fit. Drizzle with the marinara sauce and sprinkle with mozzarella (if using). Bake uncovered for 15–20 minutes, or until the eggplant is tender and the cheese is melted. Garnish with fresh basil before serving.

No-Meat Neatballs

Almond flour–based "meatballs" may sound odd and hard to make, but almond flour makes it easy to pull together protein-packed vegan meatballs in a matter of minutes! Try doubling a batch of these neatballs, freezing them, and serving them in all your favorite meatball recipes: in barbecue sauce as an appetizer, on top of **CREAMY DREAMY STROGANOFF (PAGE 155)** *or* **ALMOND MILK ALFREDO (156)** *or simply alongside spaghetti with your favorite marinara sauce. These neatballs work anywhere meatballs do—that's what makes them so "neat."*

4 cups blanched almond flour

2 tablespoons flaxseed meal

1 tablespoon nutritional yeast (optional)

1 teaspoon Italian seasoning

½ teaspoon garlic powder

1 onion, finely chopped

½ cup vegetable broth

4 tablespoons tomato paste

4 tablespoons soy sauce, tamari, or Bragg Liquid Aminos

2 tablespoons avocado, grapeseed, or olive oil

1. Preheat the oven to 350°F.
2. In a food processor, pulse together the almond flour, flaxseed meal, nutritional yeast, Italian seasoning, and garlic powder. Add the onion, vegetable broth, tomato paste, and soy sauce. Pulse until a dough forms.
3. Roll the dough into 1-inch balls and place them in a 9 × 13-inch baking dish.
4. Drizzle them with olive oil and bake for 15–20 minutes, or until neatballs are hot and light golden brown on top. Serve immediately, or freeze the cooked neatballs and keep for future use in your favorite dishes. They will store in the fridge for up to 4 days and in the freezer for up to 1 month.

gL **gR** **nL** **VE** **VT**

**MAKES
APPROXIMATELY
24 NEATBALLS**

**PER SERVING
(6 NEATBALLS)**

Calories: 440

Calories from Fat: 93

Total Fat: 4g, 6%

Saturated Fat: 1g, 5%

Total Carb: 87g, 29%

Dietary Fiber: 6g, 24%

Sugars: 3g

Protein: 14g

Cholesterol: 0mg, 0%

Sodium: 866mg, 36%

Primal Power Meatballs

*Just like the vegan **NO-MEAT NEATBALLS** recipe on **PAGE 150**, these gluten-free, protein-packed, paleo-friendly meatballs taste great atop the **CREAMY DREAMY STROGANOFF (PAGE 155)** or **ALMOND MILK ALFREDO (156)**. Serve with marinara sauce spooned on top of steamed spaghetti squash or as a great party appetizer when drizzled with a little melted butter, smoked paprika, and chopped scallions.*

MAKES APPROXIMATELY 36 MEATBALLS

2 cloves garlic, chopped
3 tablespoons chopped onion
3 eggs
1 tablespoon Italian seasoning
1 ½ teaspoons sea salt
2 pounds ground beef or ground veal
½ cup blanched almond flour

PER SERVING (6 MEATBALLS)

Calories: 256
Calories from Fat: 114
Total Fat: 12.6g, 19%
Saturated Fat: 3.1g, 16%
Total Carb: 3.2g, 1%
Dietary Fiber: 1.1g, 4%
Sugars: 0.6g
Protein: 30.7g
Cholesterol: 159mg, 53%
Sodium: 559mg, 23%

1. Preheat the oven to 350°F.
2. Place the garlic, onions, eggs, Italian seasoning, and salt in a blender. Blend until pureed.
3. Pour the mixture into a large bowl and add the ground beef and almond flour. Mix together until the meat and egg mixtures are completely incorporated.
4. Roll into 1 ½-inch balls. Place the meatballs on a baking sheet lined with parchment paper. They can be placed close to each other, but not touching (this will keep your meatballs from baking together).
5. Bake for 18–22 minutes, or until the meatballs are cooked through. Remove and allow the meatballs to cool slightly and set. Serve with your favorite sauce.

Not Your Mama's Meatloaf

Mama said hers was the best, but you'll secretly win the award for best meatloaf ever with this incredible recipe made with ground turkey. Almond flour lends natural oils to this dish as it bakes, so the final meatloaf is moist and tender. One thing Mama did get right? Raising a kid who knows how to cook.

MAKES 6 SERVINGS

**PER SERVING
(⅙ RECIPE)**

Calories: 397

Calories from Fat: 232

Total Fat: 25.8g, 40%

Saturated Fat:
11.0g, 55%

Sodium: 657mg,
27% Total Carb:
14.0g, 5%

Dietary Fiber: 2.3g,
9%

Sugars: 10.2g

Protein: 33.8g

Cholesterol: 139mg,
46%

Sodium: 657mg, 27%

FOR THE MEATLOAF

2 pounds ground turkey

1 large egg

1 onion, finely diced

1 small carrot, shredded

1 stalk of celery, finely diced

1 cup almond milk

1 cup almond flour

1 teaspoon seasoned salt

1 teaspoon olive oil

FOR THE SAUCE

⅓ cup ketchup

3 tablespoons brown sugar

3 tablespoons prepared mustard

1 teaspoon hot sauce

1. Preheat the oven to 375°F.
2. In a large bowl mix together the turkey, egg, onion, carrot, celery, almond milk, almond flour, and salt. Grease a large rimmed baking sheet with the teaspoon of olive oil. Transfer the turkey mixture from the bowl to the sheet. Pat it into a large loaf.
3. Stir the sauce ingredients together in a small bowl, and brush it on top of the meatloaf.
4. Bake for 50 minutes, or until the edges of the meatloaf begin to slightly pull away from the edges of the baking sheet.

Vegan Lentil Neatloaf

Lentils, mushrooms, almond butter, and almond flour make a delicious base for a vegan meatloaf so good, you may never want to eat the animal version again! This recipe calls for the meatloaf to be topped with vegan barbecue sauce, but it's just as good slathered in ketchup, if that's the way yo' mama served it.

D
GL
VE
VT

4 cups cremini mushrooms

2 cups cooked lentils

1 cup quick oats (gluten-free if desired)

2 tablespoons Earth Balance

½ onion, finely chopped

2 cloves garlic, chopped

½ cup raw almond butter

½ cup blanched almond flour

2 tablespoons flaxseed meal

¼ cup vegetable broth

¾ teaspoon salt

½ cup vegan barbecue sauce (optional)

MAKES 6 SERVINGS

**PER SERVING
(⅙ RECIPE)**

Calories: 481

Calories from Fat: 161

Total Fat: 16g 25%

Saturated Fat: 3g 15%

Total Carb: 62g, 21%

Dietary Fiber: 23g, 92%

Sugars: 9g

Protein: 24g

Cholesterol: 10mg, 3%

Sodium: 619mg, 26%

1. Preheat the oven to 350°F.
2. Place the mushrooms, lentils, and oats in a food processor and pulse until very, very finely chopped.
3. Heat the Earth Balance in a large skillet over medium-high heat. Add the mushroom mixture, onion, and garlic to the skillet and stir with a spatula as the mushrooms cook until softened, about 3–4 minutes.
4. Transfer the mixture to a large bowl and stir in the almond butter, almond flour, flaxseed meal, and vegetable broth. Add salt and mix until combined into a well-incorporated dough.
5. Transfer the dough into a 9 × 5-inch loaf pan sprayed with nonstick cooking spray. Spread vegan barbecue sauce or the sauce from **NOT YOUR MAMA'S MEATLOAF (PAGE 152)** atop the meatloaf, if desired.
6. Bake for 45–50 minutes or until the edges are deep brown. Remove and allow the loaf to sit for 10 minutes before turning it out of the pan and slicing.

Almond Butter Browned Steak

Steak doesn't need much to taste as good as it does at fine restaurants. Here, the rich flavors of almonds and butter come together in a quick and easy sauce that makes for a stunning main dish.

¼ cup sliced almonds

4 (8-ounce) steaks

½ teaspoon sea salt

½ teaspoon freshly ground pepper

6 tablespoons butter

1 clove garlic, chopped

3 tablespoons almond butter

1 tablespoon chopped fresh parsley

1. Heat a large skillet over medium heat. Toss the almonds into the skillet and stir with a wooden spoon until light golden brown. Remove from the skillet and set aside.
2. Dry the steaks with paper towels and sprinkle them with salt and pepper.
3. Melt 2 tablespoons of the butter in the skillet and cook the steaks for 4–5 minutes on one side, flip and cook on the second side with the pan covered for 2–3 minutes for medium rare. Cook an additional minute for medium, and another 2–3 minutes for well done. Transfer the steaks to a serving platter.
4. Place the remaining butter and the chopped garlic into the skillet, and whisk constantly until the butter begins to bubble and brown. Immediately remove the skillet from the heat, and whisk in the almond butter and sliced toasted almonds. Spoon the sauce over the steaks and sprinkle with parsley.

MAKES 4 SERVINGS

PER SERVING (1 STEAK)

Calories: 434

Calories from Fat: 281

Total Fat: 31.2g, 48%

Saturated Fat: 13.2g, 66%

Total Carb: 3.7g, 1%

Dietary Fiber: 1.2g, 5%

Sugars: 1g

Protein: 34.8g

Cholesterol: 122mg, 41%

Sodium: 396mg, 16%

Creamy Dreamy Stroganoff

Though you can serve this stroganoff over egg noodles or gluten-free pasta, my favorite way to eat it is over sweet potatoes with wilted spinach. It's a nutrient-dense way to enjoy dinner without dairy, meat, or wheat, and the colors look absolutely divine on your dinner table. Though baby bella mushrooms are specified here, feel free to use white or cremini mushrooms, as well.

6 tablespoons butter, Earth Balance, or Coconut oil

½ medium onion, finely chopped

3 cloves garlic, finely chopped

4 cups sliced baby bella mushrooms

2 tablespoons arrowroot powder or cornstarch

2 ½ cups unsweetened almond milk

1 teaspoon sea salt

1 teaspoon freshly ground pepper

12 cups baby spinach, washed

6 sweet potatoes, baked until tender

½ cup chopped Italian parsley

(D) (gL) (gR) (pL) (vE) (vT)

MAKES 6 SERVINGS

**PER SERVING
(⅙ RECIPE)**

Calories: 311

Calories from Fat: 138

Total Fat: 14g, 22%

Saturated Fat: 9g, 45%

Total Carb: 40g, 13%

Dietary Fiber: 6g, 24%

Sugars: 12g

Protein: 9g

Cholesterol: 38mg, 13%

Sodium: 677mg, 28%

1. In a large skillet, melt 5 tablespoons of the butter and cook the onion and two of the garlic cloves over medium-high heat until the onions begin to soften, about 2 minutes. Add the mushrooms and sauté until softened, about 3–4 minutes. Sprinkle the arrowroot powder over the mushrooms and add ½ cup of the almond milk to the pan. Use a spatula or wooden spoon to stir the milk into the mushrooms and mix it with the arrowroot powder. Add the remaining almond milk, salt, and pepper to the skillet and continue to stir until the sauce is warm and thickened slightly. Transfer sauce to a serving dish and wipe the skillet clean with a paper towel.

2. Melt the remaining butter in the skillet. Add the third clove of garlic and spinach, cover the skillet, and allow the spinach to wilt for 1–2 minutes.

3. Slice the sweet potatoes lengthwise, and spoon the spinach into the center of each sweet potato. Top with the mushroom stroganoff. Garnish with chopped parsley, if desired.

Almond Milk Alfredo

Pasta lovers, unite! This simple alfredo sauce takes the cream and cheese out of the classic version but retains so much flavor, you won't miss all the fat! Gluten-free eaters will want to serve this over g-free pasta. If you're watching your carb content, or just want to boost the veggies in your life, try spooning this sauce over spaghetti squash or zucchini ribbons and serving it with the **NO-MEAT NEATBALLS (PAGE 150)**.

4 tablespoons butter or Earth Balance

1 shallot, finely chopped

2 ½ tablespoons arrowroot powder or cornstarch

1 cup vegetable stock

2 cups unsweetened almond milk

2 tablespoons nutritional yeast

16 ounces fettuccine, cooked

¼ teaspoon ground nutmeg

½ teaspoon salt

1 teaspoon freshly ground pepper

¼ cup chopped Italian parsley

1. In a large skillet over medium-high heat, melt the butter and shallots together until the shallots are softened and aromatic, about 2 minutes.
2. In a small bowl, whisk together the arrowroot powder and vegetable stock, then pour it into the skillet. Whisk in the almond milk and nutritional yeast. Cook it just until the sauce thickens and is steamy. If you're using cornstarch, whisk just until the sauce begins to boil and thicken.
3. Remove from the heat and serve it over the fettuccine. Sprinkle with nutmeg, salt, and freshly ground pepper to taste. Garnish with chopped parsley.

MAKES 6 SERVINGS

**PER SERVING
(⅙ RECIPE, SAUCE ONLY)**

Calories: 475

Calories from Fat: 105

Total Fat: 11.7g, 18%

Saturated Fat: 5.3g, 27%

Total Carb: 75.6g, 25%

Dietary Fiber: 1.4g, 5%

Sugars: 0g

Protein: 16.6g

Cholesterol: 114mg, 38%

Sodium: 353mg, 15%

WHAT IS NUTRITIONAL YEAST?

Nutritional yeast, aka "nooch," is often used in vegan cooking to create a cheese-like flavor. It can be found in the bulk bins of most health food stores and is relatively inexpensive, especially because a little goes a long way. A tablespoon or two of nooch added to a recipe can lend a tremendous amount of flavor and a bit of natural orange or yellow color, as well. It's a natural source of eighteen amino acids and is also a complete protein.

A dried, deactivated fungus, nutritional yeast doesn't work like baking yeast and has no leavening ability. Because it hails from the fungi family—like mushrooms—it's safe for vegan, paleo, and gluten-free eaters alike. Try stirring it into sauces, sprinkling it on popcorn, or mixing it into mashed potatoes or mac and cheese to give your recipes a natural, cheesy flavor.

To store nooch, keep it in an airtight container in a cool, dry place. Properly stored, it will stay fresh for up to one year.

Almond Butter Pesto

Buying pine nuts for pesto can get pricey. Why buy an extra ingredient when you've got a perfectly delicious pesto sauce starter sitting right in your pantry? This recipe can be made with raw or roasted almond butter, but roasted is my favorite. It adds a depth of flavor, but raw almond butter whips into a beautiful pesto, as well. Though this recipe makes a sauce for pasta, paleo eaters will love it atop roasted cauliflower. This sauce also works nicely as a marinade and finishing sauce for steak, salmon, and chicken.

2 cups fresh basil leaves (well packed)

¼ cup almond butter

2 cloves garlic

1 tablespoon nutritional yeast (or ¼ cup shredded parmesan)

½ cup olive oil

Juice and zest of 1 lemon

½ teaspoon sea salt

6 cups cooked pasta

1. In a food processor or industrial-strength blender, pulse the basil, almond butter, garlic, nutritional yeast, olive oil, lemon juice and zest, and salt together until pureed into a grainy sauce. Drizzle it over cooked pasta, steamed veggies, or roasted cauliflower and enjoy.

D
gR
pL
VE
VT

MAKES 6 SERVINGS

**PER SERVING
(⅙ RECIPE,
PESTO ONLY)**

Calories: 588

Calories from Fat: 232

Total Fat: 25.8g, 40%

Saturated Fat: 3.4g, 17%

Total Carb: 73.2, g24%

Dietary Fiber: 1.0g, 4%

Sugars: 1g

Protein: 17.8g

Cholesterol: 93mg, 31%

Sodium: 191mg, 8%

Lazy Day Udon Noodles

A rich, creamy sauce sits atop giant, slurpy udon noodles, and a stack of fresh-cooked shiitake mushrooms completes this easy-to-make vegan dish. Serve with a glass of sake and a fortune cookie, and you've got yourself an easy-peasy meal in a matter of minutes!

D
gL
vE
vT

2 (7.2-ounce) packets precooked udon noodles

1 teaspoon sesame oil

1 tablespoon olive oil

2 cups fresh shiitake mushrooms

2 tablespoons almond butter

1 garlic clove, chopped

1 tablespoon finely grated fresh ginger

2 tablespoons soy sauce

1 cup chicken stock or vegetable broth

¼ cup thinly cut red bell pepper strips

¼ cup sliced scallions, cut on the bias

1 tablespoon sesame seeds

MAKES 6 SERVINGS

PER SERVING (⅙ RECIPE)

Calories: 347

Calories from Fat: 109

Total Fat: 12.2g, 19%

Saturated Fat: 1.3g, 7%

Total Carb: 51.4g, 17%

Dietary Fiber: 5.5g, 22%

Sugars: 8.2g

Protein: 12.2g

Cholesterol: 0mg, 0%

Sodium: 1,478mg, 62%

1. Cook the udon noodles according to the package directions. Drain and place them in a large bowl.
2. Heat the sesame and olive oil in a large skillet over medium-high heat. Toss the mushrooms into hot oil and cook until golden brown, about 2–3 minutes. Add the almond butter, garlic, ginger, soy sauce, and chicken stock to skillet. Stir it until the sauce is creamy and hot, about 2–3 minutes.
3. Drizzle the sauce over udon noodles. Top with the mushrooms. Garnish with the pepper strips, scallions, and sesame seeds.

Fiery Soba Noodles

Feisty, fiery, and full of flavor, these soba noodles are a fun way to get a vegan dish on your table, without everyone feeling like a bunny rabbit. The flavor of this sauce is reminiscent of a mild Pad Thai sauce, so if you like Thai food, you're about to find a new favorite recipe.

D
GL
VE
VT

8 ounces soba noodles

1 cup broccoli florets

1 ½ tablespoons olive oil

2 garlic cloves or shallots, minced

4 scallions (white and green parts), sliced thinly with white and green slices separated

½ tablespoon grated fresh ginger

½ cup sliced red bell pepper

½ cup sliced orange bell pepper

3 tablespoons almond butter

3 tablespoons soy sauce, tamari, or Bragg Liquid Aminos

½ teaspoon sesame oil

A few dashes of Mongolian Fire Oil or a pinch of red pepper flakes or cayenne

MAKES 6 SERVINGS

PER SERVING (⅙ RECIPE)

Calories: 345

Calories from Fat: 119

Total Fat: 13.2g, 20%

Saturated Fat: 1.6g, 8%

Total Carb: 49.2g, 16%

Dietary Fiber: 1.7g, 7%

Sugars: 1.6g

Protein: 13.2g

Cholesterol: 0mg, 0%

Sodium: 1214mg, 51%

1. Cook the soba noodles according to the package directions. Drain and run them under cold water to stop them from continuing to cook.

2. Bring a small saucepan of salted water to a boil and add the broccoli florets. Cook for 2 minutes and place the broccoli in a bowl of ice water to keep it from cooking. Drain them and set aside.

3. Heat the olive oil in a large skillet or wok until hot but not smoking. Add the garlic, whites of the scallions, and the ginger to the oil. Stir constantly until it's fragrant (about 1 minute). Add the broccoli. Sauté for 1 minute and add the peppers. Cook for 2–3 minutes or until the vegetables soften. Turn off the heat and add the soba noodles.

4. Place the almond butter, soy sauce, sesame oil, half of the green scallions, and the Mongolian Fire Oil in a food processor fitted with a metal blade. Process until smooth. Add up to ¼ cup water, depending on the consistency, and process again. Toss with the stir-fried vegetables and noodles. Garnish with the remaining green scallions.

Stealthy Healthy Mac and Cheese

This recipe was originally created for a high-speed blender. If you have one at home, it makes quick work of the meal prep, because you can puree the sauce in the blender until warm, pour it on your pasta, and voilà! Dinner is served. Don't have an industrial-strength blender? You can still puree everything in a blender, then transfer it to a saucepan for heating.

GL
VE
VT

MAKES 6 SERVINGS

**PER SERVING
(⅙ RECIPE)**

Calories: 335

Calories from Fat: 78

Total Fat: 8.6g, 13%

Saturated Fat: 1.6g, 8%

Total Carb: 51.5g, 17%

Dietary Fiber: 6.0g, 24%

Sugars: 1.8g

Protein: 14.0g

Cholesterol: 0mg, 0%

Sodium: 317mg, 13%

2 tablespoons Earth Balance

1 garlic clove, finely chopped

1 ½ tablespoons raw almond butter

1 teaspoon Dijon mustard

1 ½ tablespoons tamari, soy sauce, or Bragg Liquid Aminos

1 ⅓ cups unflavored almond milk

2 tablespoons arrowroot powder

⅓ cup nutritional yeast

⅔ cup pumpkin puree

Freshly ground pepper

6 cups cooked macaroni pasta

1. While your macaroni is cooking, melt the Earth Balance in a large saucepan over medium-high heat. Toss the garlic into the hot butter, cook for about 1 minute, then whisk in the mustard and tamari.

2. In a small bowl, whisk together the almond milk and arrowroot powder. Slowly add the milk to the hot saucepan, whisking constantly until the sauce thickens. Whisk in the nutritional yeast flakes.

3. Pour this hot sauce into a high-speed blender. Add the pumpkin. Blend on high speed for 2 minutes, until pureed and steamy.

4. Pour the sauce immediately over the cooked macaroni noodles. Pepper generously. Add salt, if needed to flavor.

Fried Chickpea Salad

Fried chickpeas had a room full of blogger friends raving with delight during a cooking contest I took part in a few years back. Since then, it's been one of my favorite ways to put an inexpensive dish on the dinner table. Frying chickpeas coats them in a crunchy outer crust, and prepared this way, they lend an almost nutty texture to salads. If you like the taste of wasabi, feel free to toss a bit of wasabi powder on top of your chickpeas, but don't panic if you don't have that ingredient in the pantry.

1 can chickpeas, drained

¼ cup blanched almond flour

1 teaspoon wasabi powder (optional)

½ teaspoon salt

1 tablespoon olive oil

4 cups arugula

4 cups chopped Bibb lettuce

1 large carrot, peeled and shredded

1 cucumber, julienned

4 scallions, diced

1 ½ cups very fresh bean sprouts

½ cup salted cashews

½ avocado

½ cup olive oil

⅓ cup rice vinegar

½ tablespoon tamari or Bragg Liquid Aminos

Juice of 2 limes

1 tablespoon almond butter

1 clove garlic

1. Coat chickpeas with almond flour, wasabi powder, and salt. Fry in 1 tablespoon olive oil heated to medium-high in a skillet.
2. Toss the arugula and lettuce with the carrots, cucumber, scallions, and bean sprouts. Top with cashews and chickpeas.
3. In a blender, combine the avocado, olive oil, vinegar, tamari, lime juice, almond butter, and garlic. Blend until pureed.
4. Drizzle the dressing over the salad just before serving.

gL gR vE vT

MAKES 4 SERVINGS

**PER SERVING
(¼ RECIPE)**

Calories: 406

Calories from Fat: 345

Total Fat: 38.3g, 59%

Saturated Fat: 5.7 g, 29%

Total Carb: 12.3g, 4%

Dietary Fiber: 7.0g, 28%

Sugars: 2.7g

Protein: 12.2g

Cholesterol: 0mg, 0%

Sodium: 599mg, 25%

Chopped Chicken Salad with Creamy Asian Almond Dressing

Toss together this simple salad and serve it with the Creamy Asian Almond Dressing. If you're a fan of Asian-flavored dressings, this creamy salad dressing will surely become a favorite. Use roasted almond butter in this recipe for a savory dressing with mild sweetness. Toss it into a coleslaw mix with fresh fried wonton wrappers, serve it as a dipping sauce for the **CRISPY CHICK'N ALMOND NUGGETS (PAGE 142),** *or drizzle it over our recipe for Chopped Chicken Salad. If you're not a fan of sesame oil, feel free to omit it. If you like things spicy, substitute hot pepper oil for the sesame oil. Don't have rice vinegar? Swap in apple cider or white vinegar, instead.*

FOR THE SALAD

6 cups chopped romaine lettuce

1 cup chopped purple cabbage

½ cup grated carrots

½ cup chopped scallions

2 cups shredded chicken breast or vegan chicken tenders

2 tablespoons toasted almonds

1 avocado, sliced

FOR THE DRESSING

¼ cup avocado or grapeseed oil

1 tablespoon sesame oil (optional)

¼ cup rice vinegar

¼ cup creamy almond butter

3 tablespoons soy sauce

2 tablespoons honey or agave nectar

1. To make the salad: In a large bowl, mix together the lettuce, cabbage, carrots, scallions, and chicken. Serve in salad bowls topped with avocado slices and toasted almonds. Drizzle with **CREAMY ASIAN ALMOND DRESSING.** Serve immediately.

MAKES 12, ½-CUP SERVINGS

PER SERVING (½ CUP SALAD)

Calories: 165

Calories from Fat: 158

Total Fat: 11g, 17%

Saturated Fat: 1g, 5%

Total Carb: 11g, 4%

Dietary Fiber: 4g, 16%

Sugars: 6g

Protein: 8g

Cholesterol: 15mg, 5%

Sodium: 50mg, 2%

2. To make the dressing: In a blender, combine the avocado oil, sesame oil, vinegar, almond butter, soy sauce, and honey. Puree the mixture until smooth. Drizzle the dressing over the salad. Serve immediately or store the salad, undressed, in an airtight container in the fridge for up to one week.

Steak Salad with Tomatoes, Scallions, and Ginger-Almond Vinaigrette

Steak salad makes a great meal every season of the year! In this recipe, arugula and tomatoes pair with almond butter and ginger for a surprisingly zesty flavor combo that makes for truly terrific eating.

1 pound hanger steak

Kosher salt

Freshly ground pepper

¼ cup olive oil

2 tablespoons red wine vinegar

2 tablespoons creamy almond butter

½ teaspoon dried ginger

4 cups roughly chopped arugula

½ cup halved orange tomatoes

½ cup halved red tomatoes

4 scallions (white and green parts), finely chopped

1. Preheat a grill to medium high. Sprinkle both sides of the steak with kosher salt and a liberal dusting of pepper. Grill for 5–7 minutes per side for medium rare.
2. While the steak is grilling, whisk together the olive oil, vinegar, almond butter, and ginger. Season to taste with salt and pepper.
3. When the steak is done, let it rest for 5 minutes and then slice it into thin pieces across the grain.
4. In a large bowl toss the arugula, tomatoes, and scallions. Top them with the steak slices and pour the vinaigrette over the steak.

MAKES 4 SERVINGS

PER SERVING (¼ RECIPE)

Calories: 332

Calories from Fat: 189

Total Fat: 21.0g, 32%

Saturated Fat: 3.5g, 18%

Total Carb: 3.6g, 1%

Dietary Fiber: 1.8g, 7%

Sugars: 1.3g

Protein: 33.3g

Cholesterol: 77mg, 26%

Sodium: 113mg, 5%

Parmesan-Crusted Tilapia

Tilapia is a mild white fish, perfect for feeding to finicky eaters or people who typically don't like fish. This tilapia, coated with a crispy Parmesan topping, tastes great when served with Italian flavors. Spaghetti squash topped with marinara would pair perfectly, or enjoy this dish with **MASHED CAULIFLOWER (PAGE 101)** *topped with fresh tomatoes and basil—a perfect flavor pairing with this delicate, delightful fish. Paleo eaters avoiding dairy will love this recipe when made with nutritional yeast instead of Parmesan—a simple substitute that still gives the final dish tons of flavor.*

1 teaspoon garlic powder

1 cup blanched almond flour

½ teaspoon salt

1 cup grated Parmesan or ¼ cup nutritional yeast

2 tablespoons avocado or olive oil

4 tilapia fillets

4 lemon wedges

1 tablespoon fresh basil or parsley for garnish (optional)

1. Preheat the oven to 350°F.
2. In a small bowl, stir together the garlic powder, almond flour, salt, and Parmesan.
3. Use a basting brush to lightly coat both sides of each fish fillet with oil. Press the fish into the almond flour mixture, flip, and coat the second side.
4. Transfer the fish to a baking sheet lined with parchment paper. Bake for 9–13 minutes, or just until the fish flakes easily with a fork. Serve immediately, garnished with lemon wedges and sprinkled with basil.

D
gL
gR
pL

MAKES 4 SERVINGS

PER SERVING (1 FILLET)

Calories: 195

Calories from Fat: 69

Total Fat: 7.7g, 12%

Saturated Fat: 4.5g, 23%

Total Carb: 2.6g, 1%

Dietary Fiber: 0.6g, 2%

Sugars: 1g

Protein: 30.3g

Cholesterol: 75mg, 25%

Sodium: 591mg, 25%

Almond-Crusted Salmon

Simple is so often splendid. Such is the case with this delicious salmon. It's dairy-free, gluten-free, and cooks up with a beautiful crunch thanks to a savory almond flour crust. Try serving this recipe with the **MARINATED SPICY KALE SALAD (PAGE 105).**

D
gL
gR

1 tablespoon olive oil

½ shallot, finely chopped

Juice and zest of 1 lime

2 tablespoons whole-grain mustard

½ tablespoon honey

½ cup almond meal

4 (4-ounce) salmon fillets

¼ teaspoon sea salt

1. Preheat the oven to 350°F.
2. In a small bowl, whisk together the oil, shallot, lime juice and zest, mustard, and honey.
3. Spread sauce on top of each salmon fillet. Press the top of the salmon into the almond meal. Sprinkle with sea salt.
4. Transfer it to a parchment-lined baking sheet and bake for 11–15 minutes, or until the fish flakes easily with a fork. Remove from the parchment and serve immediately.

MAKES 4 SERVINGS

**PER SERVING
(1 FILLET)**

Calories: 313

Calories from Fat: 150

Total Fat: 19g, 29%

Saturated Fat: 2g, 10%

Total Carb: 9g, 3%

Dietary Fiber: 3g, 12%

Sugars: 3g

Protein: 30g

Cholesterol: 66mg, 22%

Sodium: 330mg, 14%

Salmon with Cream Sauce and Scallions

Salmon makes a simple, filling weeknight meal. Slathered in this beautiful almond butter cream sauce, it's a true feast for the eyes and belly. Try pairing it with steamed broccoli, since the sauce is good enough to share over everything on your plate.

D
gL
gR

¼ cup almond butter

¼ cup tamari

¼ cup plain almond milk

2 tablespoons roughly chopped fresh basil

2 tablespoons rice vinegar or white vinegar

2 tablespoons lime juice

1 scallion, chopped

1 tablespoon grated ginger

2 tablespoons brown sugar

½ teaspoon red pepper flakes

2 tablespoons olive oil

4 (4-ounce) salmon fillets

Kosher salt

Freshly ground pepper

MAKES 4 SERVINGS

PER SERVING (1 FILLET)

Calories: 588

Calories from Fat: 366%

Total Fat: 40.6g, 63%

Saturated Fat: 6.6g, 33%

Total Carb: 10.3g, 3%

Dietary Fiber: 1.2g, 5%

Sugars: 4.7g

Protein: 44.1g

Cholesterol: 112mg, 37%

Sodium: 220mg, 9%

1. Preheat the oven to 400°F.
2. In a food processor fitted with a metal blade, pulse together the almond butter, tamari, almond milk, basil, vinegar, lime juice, scallion, ginger, brown sugar, and pepper flakes.
3. Grease a large rimmed sheet pan with 1 tablespoon of olive oil. Brush the salmon on both sides with the remaining olive oil. Season to taste with salt and pepper. Bake for 10–15 minutes, or until the salmon flakes easily with a fork.
4. Serve the salmon with the almond butter cream sauce.

Quick Coconut Shrimp

Looking for the fastest meal ever? This recipe may just win the race! Whisk, dip, and bake. That's how easy it is to pull this recipe together. It pairs perfectly with rice or **ALMOND FLOUR POLENTA (PAGE 103)** *and tastes delicious as a dinner but works equally well as an appetizer.*

1 ½ tablespoons soy sauce, tamari, or Bragg's Liquid Aminos

2 tablespoons creamy roasted almond butter

2 tablespoons raw honey

1 tablespoon coconut oil, melted

1 pound shrimp, raw with tail on

½ cup finely shredded coconut, toasted

1 teaspoon finely chopped fresh cilantro

1. Preheat the oven to 350°F.
2. In a small bowl, whisk together the soy sauce, almond butter, honey, and coconut oil.
3. Dry the shrimp with a paper towel and dip them into the almond butter mixture. Roll them in the toasted coconut and place them on a parchment-lined baking dish.
4. Bake for 9–12 minutes, or just until the shrimp turns pink and curls. Remove it from the oven and cool for a minute or two before sprinkling with cilantro and serving.

MAKES 4 SERVINGS

PER SERVING (¼ RECIPE)

Calories: 283

Calories from Fat: 114

Total Fat: 12.7g, 19%

Saturated Fat: 6.9g, 34%

Total Carb: 13.8g, 5%

Dietary Fiber: 1.9g, 8%

Sugars: 10.1g

Protein: 28.7g

Cholesterol: 239mg, 80%

Sodium: 645mg, 27%

TIP: Toasting Coconut

There are two easy ways to get perfectly toasted coconut. Make several cups at a time, then store it in airtight containers in your pantry for those moments when toasted coconut is called for in recipes.

Pan Toast

Place 1 cup shredded coconut in a large, nonstick skillet heated to medium heat. Stir constantly with a spatula, just until the edges of some of the flakes turn golden brown. Remove from the heat, transfer to a bowl, and allow to cool before storing.

Oven Toast

Preheat the oven to 325°F. Spread 1 cup of shredded coconut in a parchment-lined 8 × 8-inch baking dish. Place in the oven and bake for 6–8 minutes, stirring every minute until the coconut is light golden brown. Remove it immediately from the oven and transfer to a bowl. Allow it to cool before storing

Korean Lettuce Wraps

Korean red pepper flakes can be found in Asian grocery stores and is nice to have in the pantry. The bright red flakes add a bit of heat, but not as much as you might suspect when first spooning big, bright scarlet flakes of red pepper. Typically, it's purchased in extra large quantities, so if you're new to this recipe and not sure if you're a fan of Korean food or kimchi spices, feel free to omit the red pepper flakes and add ½ teaspoon paprika, ¼ teaspoon cayenne, and ½ teaspoon red pepper flakes, instead. Vegan and vegetarian eaters can swap the steak for black beans or vegan ground crumbles and still enjoy the goodness of this dish.

3 tablespoons white vinegar

3 tablespoons honey or sugar

¼ teaspoon salt

½ cucumber, peeled and finely sliced

¼ red onion, finely sliced

2 tablespoons avocado or coconut oil

1 clove garlic, finely chopped

1-inch piece fresh ginger, grated

1 pound flank steak, sliced thin, or 1 ½ cups meatless crumbles

½ cup soy sauce

2 tablespoons creamy almond butter

2 tablespoons Korean red pepper flakes

1 tablespoon sesame oil

6 Bibb lettuce leaves

1 tablespoon sliced scallions

D
gR
DL
vE
vT

MAKES 6 SERVINGS

**PER SERVING
(1 WRAP)**

Calories: 333

Calories from Fat: 138

Total Fat: 15.3g, 24%

Saturated: Fat 3.8g, 19%

Total Carb: 22.2g, 7%

Dietary Fiber: 3.0g, 12%

Sugars: 16.0g

Protein: 28.7g

Cholesterol: 47mg, 16%

Sodium: 2030mg, 85%

1. In a small bowl, whisk together the vinegar, 1 tablespoon of the honey, and the salt. Add the cucumber and onion slices to the bowl. Set aside.

2. In a large skillet, heat the avocado oil over medium-high heat. Add the garlic and ginger. Cook them until softened, about 1 minute. Add the steak and cook until browned, about 3–4 minutes. Add the soy sauce, almond butter, pepper

flakes, remaining honey, and sesame oil to the skillet. Stir until the steak, or thawed meatless crumbles, is coated, then immediately remove from heat.

3. Serve the steak in the Bibb lettuce leaves topped with the cucumber mixture. Garnish with sliced scallions, if desired.

10

Dessert

Whether you're looking for sweet ways to end an evening of entertaining, or simply craving a homemade chocolate chip cookie, this chapter pulls together classic recipes and new recipes that feature almond milk, almond butter, and almond flour in desserts you'll want to dive into again and again.

Usually almond flour can't be swapped teaspoon-for-teaspoon in baked goods, but it can be the only flour you bake with. Almond butter can be swapped in for peanut butter, but not always. And, almond milk works similarly to milk or cream, but how do you know which recipes will come out right? Take all the guesswork out of baking with this chapter full of sweets and treats featuring almond flour, almond butter, and almond milk.

Most of the recipes in this chapter can be easily tailored to fit gluten-free, paleo, and vegan diets. If you follow one of those eating plans, here are a few notes to help you navigate with panache.

Vegan. Swap in agave nectar, pure maple syrup, or even pure cane sugar in place of raw honey to keep these recipes plant-friendly.

Paleo. When agave nectar or pure maple syrup is called for in a recipe, use raw honey instead. Recipes calling for sugar should be avoided, and recipes with chocolate chips are not supported by strict paleo eaters, but are okay for primal eaters.

Gluten-Free. When using cornstarch, oats, cocoa powder, sprinkles, or powdered sugar, check the labeling on the package to ensure the products are gluten-free.

No-Bake Almond Butter Pears

These easy, elegant pears are perfect for dinner parties full of health-conscious eaters. If anyone's gluten-free, vegan, raw, or paleo-friendly, a few minor tweaks will make this recipe work for everyone in your crowd. For a paleo version, omit the cream cheese, double the almond butter, and use honey instead of maple syrup. Take this recipe raw by omitting the cream cheese and using raw almond butter and raw honey or maple syrup. Vegan cream cheese and maple syrup work best for plant-based foodies.

3 pears

¼ cup almond butter

¼ cup mascarpone, cream cheese, or vegan cream cheese

1 teaspoon apple pie spice

3 tablespoons raw honey or maple syrup

2 tablespoons chopped toasted almonds

1. Cut the pears in half. Use a spoon or melon baller to remove the center pit of each pear.
2. In a small bowl, beat the almond butter, cream cheese, and apple pie spice together until smooth.
3. Spoon the mixture into the center of each pear. Drizzle with honey and top with chopped almonds.

MAKES 6 SERVINGS

PER SERVING (½ PEAR)

Calories: 171

Calories from Fat: 63

Total Fat: 7.0g, 11%

Saturated Fat: 0.7g, 3%

Total Carb: 27.3g, 9%

Dietary Fiber: 3.9g, 16%

Sugars: 19.0g

Protein: 3.1g

Cholesterol: 0mg, 0%

Sodium: 2mg, 0%

Three-Ingredient Almond Butter Cookies

Three ingredients are all you need to pull together these delicious almond butter cookies. Just mix, bake, and pull a pan full of hot, homemade cookies from your oven! In this recipe, no-stir roasted almond butter or no-stir roasted flavored almond butters work best. You'll want the creamy, low-oil prestirred variety to make a perfect batch of these cookies. If desired, add a half-teaspoon of baking powder to keep them extra light.

1 cup no-stir almond butter
½ cup sugar
1 egg

1. Preheat the oven to 350°F.
2. In a large bowl, combine the almond butter, sugar, and egg until well mixed.
3. Roll tablespoons of the dough into balls, place on a parchment-lined baking sheet, then flatten each cookie slightly by pressing down with the tines of a fork.
4. Bake in a preheated oven for 8–10 minutes, or just until the cookies set. Remove and let cool slightly before transferring the cookies to a cooling rack.

MAKES 8 COOKIES

PER SERVING (1 COOKIE)
Calories: 255
Calories from Fat: 164
Total Fat: 18.2g, 28%
Saturated Fat: 1.8g, 9%
Total Carb: 18.0g, 6%
Dietary Fiber: 1.2g, 5%
Sugars: 12.5g
Protein: 7.3g
Cholesterol: 20mg, 7%
Sodium: 8mg, 0%

Almond Butter Snickerdoodles

Snickerdoodles are one of the web's most searched-for cookies. It's no wonder why! The classic combo of cinnamon and sugar is easy to bake, easy to eat, and easy to love. This almond butter cookie version is so good, you'll want to eat them for breakfast, too.

⅔ cup butter, softened

1 cup sugar

2 eggs

3 cups blanched almond flour

1 tablespoon pure vanilla extract

1 tablespoon cinnamon

¾ teaspoon baking powder

¾ teaspoon salt

1. Preheat the oven to 350°F.
2. In a large bowl or stand mixer, beat together the butter, ⅔ cup of the sugar, and the eggs until light and creamy. Add the almond flour, vanilla, 1 teaspoon cinnamon, baking powder, and salt to the bowl. Beat until a soft dough forms.
3. In a small bowl, stir together the remaining sugar and cinnamon.
4. Roll tablespoon-size rounds of dough into balls, then roll in the cinnamon sugar. Place the cookies on a parchment-lined baking sheet.
5. Bake for 8–10 minutes, or until the edges turn light golden brown. Remove from oven and cool on a cooling rack.

MAKES 24 COOKIES

**PER SERVING
(1 COOKIE)**

Calories: 124

Calories from Fat: 63

Total Fat: 7.0g, 11%

Saturated Fat: 0.6g, 3%

Total Carb: 11.7g, 4%

Dietary Fiber: 1.6g, 7%

Sugars: 8.4g

Protein: 3.5g

Cholesterol: 14mg, 5%

Sodium: 84mg, 4%

Ultimate Almond Butter Chocolate Chip Cookies

Chocolate chip cookies with the addition of almond butter aren't just better tasting—they're crispy on the outside, soft on the inside, and sure to become a new favorite. The natural oils of almond butter combine with all the flavors you already love in a chocolate chip cookie to make a familiar cookie with a touch of "wow" baked inside.

1 cup almond butter

¾ cup brown sugar or ¼ cup raw honey

1 large egg

½ teaspoon baking soda

¼ teaspoon salt

½ cup dark chocolate chunks

1. Preheat the oven to 350°F.
2. In a large bowl, whisk together the almond butter, brown sugar, egg, baking soda, and salt until a soft dough forms. Stir in the dark chocolate chunks.
3. Drop the dough by the tablespoonfuls onto a parchment-lined baking sheet.
4. Bake in preheated oven for 8–10 minutes, or just until the centers of the cookies are set. Remove and cool on a cooling rack before serving with a big glass of almond milk.

MAKES 12 COOKIES

PER SERVING (1 COOKIE)

Calories: 173

Calories from: Fat 110

Total Fat: 12.2g, 19%

Saturated Fat: 1.2g, 6%

Total Carb: 12.6g, 4%

Dietary Fiber: 0.8g, 3%

Sugars: 8.8g

Protein: 4.9g

Cholesterol: 16mg, 5%

Sodium: 111mg, 5%

Pumpkin Cookies

If you're a fan of pumpkin cookies, these taste just as good as the original . . . only these come with a lot less sugar and a lot more protein. These cookies bake up soft and beautifully spiced, full of rich pumpkin flavor. Speckled with mini chocolate chips, they make a great lunchbox goodie or autumn party treat.

gL

gR

nL

vT

1 ½ cups almond flour

1 egg

4 tablespoons honey

½ cup pumpkin puree

2 tablespoons butter, melted

1 tablespoon pumpkin pie spice

½ teaspoon baking powder

¼ teaspoon salt

1 cup mini chocolate chips

1. Preheat the oven to 350°F.
2. Whisk all the ingredients together in a large bowl until well mixed.
3. Spoon dollops of the batter onto a parchment-lined baking sheet.
4. Bake for 10–14 minutes, or until the cookies have set. Cool slightly before serving.

MAKES 12 COOKIES

**PER SERVING
(1 COOKIE)**

Calories: 162

Calories from Fat: 85

Total Fat: 9.5g, 15%

Saturated Fat: 4.8g, 24%

Total Carb: 19.8g, 7%

Dietary Fiber: 1.8g, 7%

Sugars: 15.6g

Protein: 1.4g

Cholesterol: 19mg, 6%

Sodium: 72mg, 3%

No-Bake Almond Butter Cookies

Remember those no-bake cookies from childhood? They were the first cookie I learned to make and are quite a simple way to introduce kids to cooking. This recipe riffs on the original with the addition of almond butter and coconut milk—making it peanut-and dairy-free. If you're watching your sugar intake, feel free to use coconut sugar in place of the sugar for an end result that's just as good as the traditional version.

1 cup sugar

⅓ cup coconut milk

½ cup Earth Balance or butter

¾ cup creamy, no-stir almond butter

3 tablespoons cocoa

1 tablespoon pure vanilla extract

¼ teaspoon salt

2 cups quick-cooking oats (or gluten-free rolled oats)

1. In a large saucepan, bring the sugar, coconut milk, and Earth Balance to a boil.
2. Remove the mixture and stir in the almond butter, cocoa, vanilla, salt, and oats. Keep stirring until the dough thickens.
3. Drop by rounded tablespoons onto a piece of parchment paper. Allow the cookies to cool before serving. The cookies will thicken and hold together as they cool.

MAKES 12 COOKIES

**PER SERVING
(1 COOKIE)**

Calories: 154

Calories from Fat: 70

Total Fat: 7.7g, 12%

Saturated Fat: 4.9g, 24%

Total Carb: 20.4g, 7%

Dietary Fiber: 1.4g, 6%

Sugars: 12.9g

Protein: 1.7g

Cholesterol: 15mg, 5%

Sodium: 77mg, 3%

Avalanche Bars

Avalanche bars are one of those go-to recipes that you can make at the last minute. They're so good that everyone will think you're a master baker who took all day pulling these together. Keep all the ingredients on hand for those moments when you need a dessert fast, from items you already have in your pantry.

2 cups white chocolate chips
¼ cup creamy almond butter
3 cups crisp brown rice cereal
1 ½ cups mini marshmallows
⅓ cup mini dark chocolate chips + 2 tablespoons for topping

1. Place the white chocolate chips in a clean, dry microwavable bowl. Microwave on medium for 30 seconds. Stir with a clean, dry spoon, and microwave for another 30 seconds. Repeat until the chocolate has melted, approximately 2 minutes. Add the almond butter and stir until well combined.
2. Place the cereal in a large bowl and pour the white chocolate mixture over it. Gently stir until well combined and cool. Fold in the marshmallows and the ⅓ cup dark chocolate chips gently.
3. Spoon the mixture into an 8 × 8-inch pan fitted with parchment paper. Press down firmly, but not roughly—you don't want to crush the cereal. Sprinkle with the 2 tablespoons of chocolate chips. Refrigerate for an hour to set.

MAKES 16 BARS

PER SERVING (1 BAR)
Calories: 187
Calories from Fat: 93
Total Fat: 10.3g 16%
Total Carb: 22.4g 7%
Dietary Fiber: 1.0g, 4%
Sugars: 16.7g
Protein: 2.6g
Cholesterol: 4mg, 1%
Sodium: 50mg, 2%

Almond Flour Macaroons

Coconut macaroons are typically made with eggs, but this version doesn't need them. Honey and coconut oil bind the cookies together. A smidgen of almond flour and almond extract lends mouth-watering flavor. These cookies are wildly easy to make, and the filling texture of these sweet treats makes them perfect for taking along to soccer games or on long hikes, or just for sneaking nibbles as a midnight snack.

D
gL
gR
pL
vE
vT

1 ½ cups finely shredded unsweetened coconut
1 ½ tablespoons almond flour
¼ teaspoon sea salt
2 tablespoons coconut oil
¼ cup raw honey or agave nectar
¼ teaspoon almond extract

1. Preheat the oven to 325°F.
2. In a large bowl or stand mixer, beat together all the ingredients until a soft ball of dough forms. Add an extra half-tablespoon of honey, if needed, to pull the dough together.
3. Spoon the dough onto a parchment lined baking sheet. Bake for 8–12 minutes, or just until the tops of the cookies turn a very light golden brown. Remove from the oven and allow to cool completely before serving.

MAKES 12 MACAROONS

PER SERVING (1 MACAROON)

Calories: 97
Calories from Fat: 66
Total Fat: 7.4g, 11%
Saturated Fat: 5.0g, 25%
Total Carb: 8.1g, 3%
Dietary Fiber: 1.3g, 5%
Sugars: 6.6g
Protein: 1.1g
Cholesterol: 0mg, 0%
Sodium: 43mg, 2%

Flourless Chocolate Fudge Brownies

These are about to become your new favorite brownie! Made with almond flour, they're soft and moist, with the perfect ratio of fudge-like and cakey. For extra chocolate flavor, sprinkle a quarter-cup of dark chocolate chips over the batter before baking.

2 eggs

4 tablespoons butter, softened

2 tablespoons creamy almond butter

3 tablespoons raw honey or agave nectar

1 teaspoon pure vanilla extract

½ cup almond flour

⅓ cup unsweetened cocoa powder

1 teaspoon baking soda

½ teaspoon salt

1. Preheat the oven to 350°F.
2. In a large bowl or stand mixer, beat together the eggs, butter, almond butter, and honey until well mixed. Add the vanilla, almond flour, cocoa powder, baking soda, and salt. Mix until well combined.
3. Spoon the batter into an 8 × 8-inch pan sprayed with nonstick cooking spray or lined with parchment. Bake for 22–26 minutes, or until the brownies spring back when touched lightly in the center. Remove the brownies from the oven and cool before slicing into 9 servings.

MAKES 9 BROWNIES

PER SERVING (1 BROWNIE)

Calories: 125

Calories from Fat: 89

Total Fat: 9.9g, 15%

Saturated Fat: 4.0g, 20%

Total Carb: 8.9g, 3%

Dietary Fiber: 1.9g, 7%

Sugars: 6.2g

Protein: 3.4g

Cholesterol: 50mg, 17%

Sodium: 332mg, 14%

Almond Cookie Dough Truffles

If you like eating cookie dough, you're in for a treat. The center of these sweet truffles taste just like raw cookie dough. Almond butter and brown sugar blend together with vanilla-almond-caramel goodness, and turn easy-to-make truffles into easy-to-eat treats.

½ cup butter or Earth Balance

½ cup dark brown sugar

½ cup powdered sugar

1 teaspoon pure vanilla extract

¼ teaspoon salt

½ cup creamy almond butter

1 ¼ cups blanched almond flour

2 cups mini chocolate chips (for vegan, must be labeled "dairy-free")

1. In a large bowl or stand mixer, beat together the butter, brown sugar, powdered sugar, vanilla, salt, almond butter, and almond flour until a soft batter forms. Stir in ½ cup of the chocolate chips.

2. Roll the dough into 1-inch balls. Place the truffles on a piece of parchment paper and set in the freezer while preparing the melted chocolate coating.

3. Place the remaining chocolate chips in a microwave-safe glass bowl and microwave for 30 seconds. Stir with a clean, dry spoon, and microwave for another 30 seconds. Repeat until the chocolate has melted, approximately 2 minutes time.

4. Dip the truffles into the melted chocolate and place on parchment until the chocolate cools and hardens.

Truffle Pops!

Turn these truffles into Truffle Pops by dipping the tip of a sucker stick into the melted chocolate, then pressing the chocolate-dipped end of the sucker stick into the center of the truffles. Place the truffles into the freezer for 15 minutes, then remove and gently dip each truffle into the melted chocolate chips. Allow to dry on a piece of parchment before serving.

D
gL
vE
vT

MAKES 24 TRUFFLES

PER SERVING (1 TRUFFLE)

Calories: 124

Calories from Fat: 86

Total Fat: 9.5g, 15%

Saturated Fat: 2.9g, 15%

Total Carb: 7.6g, 3%

Dietary Fiber: 0.8g, 3%

Sugars: 5.4g

Protein: 2.4g

Cholesterol: 10mg, 3%

Sodium: 53mg, 2%

Baked Vanilla Donuts
with Chocolate Frosting

You'll need a donut pan to make a batch of these soft, delicious home-baked donuts. If you don't have one, bake donut muffins in mini muffin tins for 12–15 minutes.

gL
gR
pL
vT

FOR THE DONUTS

¼ cup butter or Earth Balance, softened

2 tablespoons raw honey or agave nectar

3 eggs

1 ¼ cups blanched almond flour

¼ teaspoon salt

½ teaspoon baking powder

1 tablespoon pure vanilla extract

FOR THE FROSTING

½ cup dark chocolate chips

4 tablespoons coconut oil

¼ teaspoon almond extract (optional)

½ teaspoon vanilla extract (optional)

Sprinkles for garnish, if desired

Special Equipment: One 6-count donut baking pan

MAKES 6 DONUTS

PER SERVING (1 DONUT)

Calories: 393

Calories from Fat: 294

Total Fat: 32.7g, 50%

Saturated Fat: 15.9g, 79%

Total Carb: 18.1g, 6%

Dietary Fiber: 2.5g, 10%

Sugars: 11.6g

Protein: 8.5g

Cholesterol: 102mg, 34%

Sodium: 191mg, 8%

1. Preheat the oven to 350°F.
2. To make the donuts, in a large bowl or stand mixer, beat the butter, honey, and eggs until well mixed. Add the almond flour, salt, baking powder, and vanilla. Mix just until combined.
3. Spoon the mixture into a donut pan sprayed with nonstick baking spray. Bake for 8–10 minutes, or just until the donuts spring back when touched lightly. Remove from the oven and let cool slightly before turning them out on a cooling rack.

4. While the donuts are baking, prepare the frosting by placing the chocolate chips and coconut oil together in a microwave-safe bowl. Cook in microwave for 60–90 seconds, then remove and stir until smooth. Return to the microwave for 30–60 seconds more, if needed. Cover and refrigerate for 10–15 minutes, then spoon the frosting into a stand mixer and whip until soft and fluffy. Add the almond and vanilla extracts (if using), and beat to incorporate. Frost the cooled donuts, and garnish with sprinkles if desired.

5. For paleo eaters, check out the tips on page 9 to ensure the proper recipe prep for your diet type.

TIP: Paleo Sprinkles! Paleo eaters love sprinkles, too! Use a drop of beet juice, kale juice, or turmeric to naturally tint shredded coconut with color. Sprinkle on your donuts—or most desserts—and enjoy!

Pistachio Cherry Chocolate Biscotti

Coffee drinkers, rejoice! These incredibly flavorful almond-flour biscotti call for a cup of coffee for dipping. This recipe calls for arrowroot powder, which can be found in the gluten-free section of most grocery stores. Arrowroot is a starchy tuber, used for "sticking" this recipe together. It's gluten-free, vegan-friendly, and primal approved, though some paleo eaters avoid it because of the natural starches. If you don't have arrowroot, you can swap in cornstarch (for gluten-free and vegan eaters) or add two tablespoons of coconut flour plus an extra tablespoon of honey (for paleo eaters) and still get beautiful biscotti results.

1 ¼ cups blanched almond flour

1 tablespoon arrowroot powder

¼ teaspoon sea salt

½ teaspoon baking powder

¼ cup raw honey or agave nectar

¼ teaspoon pure vanilla extract or almond extract

¼ teaspoon cinnamon

3 tablespoons dried cherries, chopped

3 tablespoons dark chocolate chunks

3 tablespoons pistachios, coarsely chopped

1. Preheat the oven to 350°F.
2. In a stand mixer or large food processor, add the almond flour, arrowroot powder, salt, and baking powder. Add honey, vanilla, and cinnamon and pulse until the dough thickens and forms a ball. Fold in the cherries, chocolate chunks, and pistachios.
3. Form dough into a large oval, about 1 ½ inch thick, and place on a parchment-lined baking sheet. Bake for 15 minutes, then remove from oven and allow to sit until cool to the touch.
4. Using a very sharp knife, slice the baked dough into twelve slices and arrange them flat on the baking sheet.
5. Lower heat to 325°F, bake biscotti for 7 minutes, then flip and bake for 5–8 minutes more, or just until they become crispy and light golden brown. Remove and cool completely before serving. Store in an airtight container for up to 1 week.

MAKES 12 BISCOTTI

**PER SERVING
(1 BISCOTTI)**

Calories: 291

Calories from Fat: 189

Total Fat: 21.0g, 32%

Saturated Fat: 2.9g, 15%

Total Carb: 20.3g, 7%

Dietary Fiber: 5.1g, 20%

Sugars: 9.8g

Protein: 9.4g

Cholesterol: 0mg, 0%

Sodium: 44mg, 2%

One-Bowl Almond Apricot Cake

One spoon, one bowl. That's all you need to make this moist and dense cake. Bright, simple, and perfect for afternoon entertaining, this dessert is also a no-fuss, not-too-sweet treat to end any meal. Honey-averse paleo bakers can swap in brown sugar instead of the honey and still yield tasty results.

6 eggs

1 cup blanched almond flour

8 tablespoons raw honey

1 teaspoon almond extract

1 teaspoon baking powder

½ teaspoon sea salt

8 ripe apricots, pitted and halved

1 cup honey-sweetened fresh whipped cream (optional)

Special Equipment: Springform pan

1. Preheat the oven to 350°F.
2. In a large bowl, whisk together the eggs, almond flour, 6 tablespoons of the raw honey, the almond extract, baking powder, and salt. Pour into a springform pan sprayed with nonstick cooking spray.
3. Press the un-cut side of the apricots into the top of the cake and drizzle the remaining honey on top. Bake in the preheated oven for 45–50 minutes or until the cake springs back when touched lightly. Remove from the oven and let cool completely before serving with fresh whipped cream, if desired.

TIP: Don't have a springform pan? Feel free to bake this cake in a 9 × 9-inch cake round. Rather than pressing the apricots onto the top of the cake, you'll set them on the bottom of the pan, cut-side down, and bake the cake like an upside-down cake. Drizzle with the honey after baking for a beautiful presentation.

MAKES 1 CAKE (8 SERVINGS)

PER SERVING (⅛ RECIPE)

Calories: 266

Calories from Fat: 141

Total Fat: 15.6g, 24%

Saturated Fat: 5.0g, 25%

Total Carb: 25.2g, 8%

Dietary Fiber: 2.2g, 9%

Sugars: 20.8g

Protein: 8.0g

Cholesterol: 143mg, 48%

Sodium: 176mg, 7%

Primal Cookie Dough Power Bars

With a texture similar to a Clif Bar, the flavor of real-life cookie dough, and the goodness of ingredients, you can take these homemade power bars on a hike or pack them in a kid's lunchbox. Store them in the fridge for up to a week and you'll always have a grab-and-go snack awaiting your hunger cravings.

1 cup almond flour

1 cup coconut flour

½ cup almond butter

3 tablespoons raw honey or agave nectar

2 tablespoons coconut oil, melted

1 teaspoon pure vanilla extract

½ teaspoon espresso powder (optional)

1 cup dark chocolate chips (for vegan, must be labeled "dairy-free")

1. In a large bowl, combine the almond flour, coconut flour, almond butter, honey, coconut oil, vanilla, and espresso powder with a fork. Once mixed, knead it together with your hands until the mixture resembles thick cookie dough. If it's too sticky, add a little more almond flour. If it's too thick, add a little more honey and melted coconut oil.

2. Stir in chocolate chips. Press the dough into a parchment-lined 9 × 9-inch baking dish. Cover it with plastic wrap and refrigerate about 30 minutes until ready to slice into 12 bars and serve.

MAKES 12 BARS

**PER SERVING
(1 BAR)**

Calories: 204

Calories from Fat: 117

Total Fat: 13.0g, 20%

Saturated Fat: 4.6g, 23%

Total Carb: 18.7g, 6%

Dietary Fiber: 4.0g, 16%

Sugars: 10.4g

Protein: 4.7g

Cholesterol: 0mg, 0%

Sodium: 21mg, 1%

Blackberry Almond Bars

Blackberries and almonds are better when they're together! These buttery crumb bars have bright blackberries baked in. Cool them completely before slicing, for best results.

¼ cup coconut oil or butter

⅓ cup honey or agave nectar

¼ cup almond butter

1 egg

½ teaspoon pure vanilla extract

1 ¼ cups almond flour

¾ teaspoon baking powder

½ teaspoon cinnamon

½ teaspoon ground ginger

½ teaspoon salt

1 ½ cups fresh or frozen blackberries

1. Preheat the oven to 350°F. In a large bowl, beat together the coconut oil, honey, almond butter, egg, and vanilla. Add the the almond flour, baking powder, cinnamon, ginger, and salt and stir until a soft batter forms.

2. Spread into an 9 × 13-inch baking dish sprayed with nonstick cooking spray. Sprinkle the blackberries on top of the batter. Bake for 13–17 minutes, or until the center springs back when touched lightly. Cool completely before slicing into 12 bars and serving.

D **gL** **gR** **pL** **vE** **vT**

MAKES 12 BARS

PER SERVING (1 BAR)

Calories: 132

Calories from Fat: 85

Total Fat: 9.4g, 14%

Saturated Fat: 4.4g, 22%

Total Carb: 11.4g, 4%

Dietary Fiber: 1.5g,6%

Sugars: 8.8g

Protein: 2.5g

Cholesterol: 14mg, 5%

Sodium: 104mg, 4%

Chocolate Almond Cupcakes with Coco-Coconut Buttercream

These chocolate almond cupcakes are sweetened without sugar and topped with a no-sugar chocolate frosting. So, are they any good? Absolutely. The cupcakes bake up soft and moist. The frosting is light and fluffy. You won't believe they were baked without wheat flour or sugar.

g **L**
g **R**
p **L**
v **T**

FOR THE CUPCAKES

2 eggs

¼ cup coconut oil, butter, or Earth Balance, softened

1 ¾ cups blanched almond flour

¼ cup cocoa powder

1 teaspoon baking powder

¼ cup almond milk

5 tablespoons honey or agave nectar

1 teaspoon pure vanilla extract

½ teaspoon almond extract (optional)

FOR THE BUTTERCREAM

1 ½ cups dark chocolate chips

⅔ cup coconut oil

¼ cup creamy no-stir almond butter

1 teaspoon pure vanilla extract

Special Equipment: Muffin tin; cupcake liners

1. Preheat the oven to 350°F. In a large bowl or stand mixer, beat the eggs until fluffy. Add the coconut oil, almond flour, cocoa powder, baking powder, almond milk, honey, vanilla, and almond extract. Beat until smooth.

2. Spoon the batter into a muffin tin lined with cupcake liners. Bake for 18–21 minutes, or just until the centers spring back when touched lightly.

**MAKES
12 CUPCAKES**

**PER SERVING
(1 CUPCAKE)**

Calories: 297

Calories from Fat: 240

Total Fat: 26.7g, 41%

Saturated Fat: 16.5g, 82%

Total Carb: 12.3g, 4%

Dietary Fiber: 2.4g, 10%

Sugars: 7.5g

Protein: 4.9g

Cholesterol: 27mg, 9%

Sodium: 18mg, 1%

3. While the cupcakes are baking, place the chocolate chips, coconut oil, almond butter, and vanilla in a microwave-safe bowl. Heat for 60–90 seconds or until the chocolate chips are melted. Stir until smooth. Cover and place the mixture in the fridge for 15–20 minutes. Remove mixture from fridge and spoon it into a stand mixer or large bowl. Beat on high until very light and fluffy. Frost cooled cupcakes and serve.

Campfire Apple Crisp

This recipe is a gluten-free, paleo-friendly, vegan-happy version of traditional apple crisp. If you don't have coconut oil, butter or Earth Balance will work just as well. Granny Smith apples yield a tangy, tasty final result, but you can use any apple in this recipe, with the exception of Red Delicious. They cook up mushier and grainer than Gala, Braeburn, Pink Lady, and good ol' Granny Smith apples.

D
gL
gR
pL
vE
vT

1 ½ cups almond flour
½ teaspoon sea salt
2 teaspoons apple pie spice
⅓ cup coconut oil
¼ cup honey or agave nectar
1 tablespoon pure vanilla extract
6 Granny Smith apples, peeled and sliced thin
Juice of 1 lemon

MAKES 6 SERVINGS

PER SERVING
(⅙ RECIPE)

Calories: 290
Calories from Fat: 141
Total Fat: 15.7g, 24%
Saturated Fat: 10.8g, 54%
Total Carb: 38.9g, 13%
Dietary Fiber: 5.2g, 21%
Sugars: 31.1g
Protein: 1.6g
Cholesterol: 0mg, 0%
Sodium: 5mg, 0%

1. Preheat the oven to 350°F.
2. In a small bowl, combine the almond flour, salt, and apple pie spice. Stir in the coconut oil, honey, and vanilla until the mixture resembles coarse crumbs.
3. Place the apples in the bottom of a 1 ½- or 2-quart baking dish. Squeeze the lemon juice over the apples. Sprinkle with the almond topping.
4. Cover and bake for 40 minutes, then remove the cover and bake for 10–15 minutes more, until the topping turns a light, golden brown.

Almond Flour Pie Crust

There are as many versions of almond flour pie crust as there are versions of pie. This is my favorite. Not only is it vegan, paleo, and gluten-free, it's easy to make. If you're not feeling too picky, feel free to press it into the bottom of a pie pan and forego the part where you chill and roll out the dough. For a prettier pie crust, you'll definitely want to follow all the steps as written.

1 ¼ cups blanched almond flour

1 tablespoon honey or pure maple syrup

½ teaspoon salt

⅓ cup coconut oil, melted

2 teaspoons ice water

1. Preheat the oven to 400°F.
2. In a medium bowl, use a fork to stir together the almond flour, honey, and salt. Stir in the coconut oil until well combined. Add 1 teaspoon of the ice water, stirring the dough together with a fork. Add the second teaspoon a little at a time, and add only enough to make the dough start sticking together.
3. Turn the dough out onto a piece of parchment paper and knead it a couple of times. Wrap the parchment around the dough and place in the fridge for 1–2 hours. Remove from the fridge and roll the dough out between two pieces of parchment, until ¼ inch thick.
4. Place in a ungreased pie tin and bake for 8–12 minutes, or until the crust turns a light, golden brown. Fill with your favorite pie filling. If you're baking a pie that requires the pie crust to bake with the filling, do not prebake the crust.

D
g^L
g^R
p^L
VE
VT

MAKES 1 PIE CRUST (8 SERVINGS)

PER SERVING (⅛ RECIPE)

Calories: 191

Calories from Fat: 157

Total Fat: 17.4g, 27%

Saturated Fat: 8.5g, 42%

Total Carb: 5.9g, 2%

Dietary Fiber: 1.9g, 8%

Sugars: 2.2g

Protein: 3.8g

Cholesterol: 0mg, 0%

Sodium: 154mg, 6%

Vanilla Almond Milk Custard Pie

This basic almond milk custard makes a base for any flavor you desire. Craving banana cream, coconut cream, or chocolate cream pie? Start here, then follow the tips for turning this basic vanilla custard into the almond milk–based cream pie of your dreams.

⅓ cup honey, agave nectar, pure maple syrup, or sugar

1 tablespoons butter, Earth Balance, or melted coconut oil

1 tablespoon pure vanilla extract

3 cups almond milk

3 ½ tablespoons arrowroot powder or ¼ cup cornstarch

¼ teaspoon salt

1 prebaked **ALMOND FLOUR PIE CRUST (PAGE 195)**

1. In a large saucepan over medium heat, whisk together the honey, butter, vanilla, and 2 cups of the almond milk. In a small bowl, whisk together the remaining 1 cup of almond milk with the arrowroot powder. Slowly add this mixture to the saucepan, whisking constantly until the custard begins to thicken. If you're thickening it with arrowroot, you don't want the custard to boil. If you're thickening it with cornstarch, the custard will need to come to a boil in order to thicken properly. You'll know when your custard is ready because it will become the consistency of pudding.

2. Remove from the stove, whisk in the salt, and allow the custard to cool before spooning into your prepared pie crust. Cover and refrigerate until chilled, about 2–3 hours.

D **gL** **gR** **pL** **vE** **vT**

**MAKES 1 PIE
(8 SERVINGS)**

**PER SERVING
(⅛ RECIPE,
CUSTARD ONLY)**

Calories: 259

Calories from Fat: 193

Total Fat: 21.5g, 33%

Saturated Fat: 19.0g, 95%

Total Carb: 17.0g, 6%

Dietary Fiber: 2.0g, 8%

Sugars: 11.5g

Protein: 2.1g

Cholesterol: 0mg, 0%

Sodium: 87mg, 4%

Custard Cream Everything

Turn this easy vanilla custard into all of your favorite cream pie fillings with a few easy mix-ins.

Banana Cream Pie: Whisk two ripe, smashed bananas and 1 tablespoon rum flavoring into the vanilla custard as soon as you remove it from the heat.

Coconut Cream Pie: Whisk 1 cup toasted, finely shredded coconut and 1 teaspoon coconut extract into the vanilla custard as soon as you remove it from the heat.

Chocolate Cream Pie: Add 3 tablespoons chocolate chips and 3 tablespoons cocoa powder to the saucepan when you add the butter and honey.

Lemon Cream Pie: Instead of the initial 2 cups almond milk, use 1 ½ cups, and before adding the arrowroot mixture, stir in ⅓ cup freshly squeezed lemon juice and 1 tablespoon fresh lemon zest (1 teaspoon lemon extract will boost the flavor even more). Heat until thickened, as per original recipe instructions.

Key Lime Cream: Instead of the initial 2 cups almond milk, use 1 ½ cups, and before adding the arrowroot mixture, stir in ⅓ cup freshly squeezed lime juice and ½ tablespoon fresh lime zest to the vanilla custard recipe. Tint with a drop or two of natural green food coloring, if desired.

Almond Milk Pumpkin Pie

Gluten-free, vegan, paleo-friendly, and perfect, this gluten-free pumpkin pie tastes like a classic but kicks out the eggs traditionally found in pumpkin pies. If preparing for a holiday meal, making this recipe the night before is strongly recommended, since it tastes best after setting up in the fridge for at least three hours.

2 cups pumpkin puree

⅓ cup raw honey or pure maple syrup

¼ cup almond milk

1 tablespoon butter or Earth Balance

3 tablespoons arrowroot powder

1 tablespoon pure vanilla extract

2 tablespoons pumpkin pie spice

1 **ALMOND FLOUR PIE CRUST (PAGE 195)**, pressed into a 9-inch pie tin, unbaked

1. Preheat the oven to 350°F.
2. In a large bowl, whisk together the pumpkin puree, honey, almond milk, butter, arrowroot powder, vanilla, and pumpkin pie spice. Pour into the pie crust.
3. Bake for 40 minutes. Cover the edges of the pie crust with tin foil and bake for another 15 minutes. Remove the pie from the oven, allow it to cool to the touch, then refrigerate it for 3 hours (or up to overnight) to allow the pie to fully set and firm up.

**MAKES 1 PIE
(8 SERVINGS)**

**PER SERVING
(⅛ RECIPE)**

Calories: 308

Calories from Fat: 189

Total Fat: 21.0g, 32%

Saturated Fat: 11.2g, 56%

Total Carb: 27.1g, 9%

Dietary Fiber: 4.1g, 16%

Sugars: 16.4g

Protein: 4.7g

Cholesterol: 4mg, 1%

Sodium: 170mg, 7%

Chocolate Layered Almond Butter Pie

This decadent recipe is like a raw almond butter mousse. Poured into a pie crust, topped with drizzled chocolate, toasted almonds, and coconut, it makes a pretty presentation and can be enjoyed by every kind of eater since it's dairy free, gluten-free, paleo-friendly, and vegan (when made with Earth Balance and agave nectar).

D
gL
gR
pL
VE
VT

**MAKES 1 PIE
(10 SERVINGS)**

2 (15-ounce) cans full-fat coconut milk that have been refrigerated overnight

1 ½ cups dark chocolate chips (for vegan, must be labeled "dairy-free")

1 **ALMOND FLOUR PIE CRUST (PAGE 195)**, baked

¾ cup no-stir almond butter

3 tablespoons butter or Earth Balance, melted

¼ cup almond milk

⅓ cup honey, agave nectar, pure maple syrup or sugar

1 tablespoon pure vanilla extract

¼ cup shredded coconut, toasted

¼ cup sliced almonds, toasted

**PER SERVING
(¹⁄₁₀ RECIPE)**

Calories: 561

Calories from Fat: 427

Total Fat: 47.5g, 73%

Saturated Fat: 25.1g, 125%

Total Carb: 30.7g, 10%

Dietary Fiber: 3.9g, 15%

Sugars: 20.1g

Protein: 10.0g

Cholesterol: 9mg, 3%

Sodium: 155mg, 6%

1. Open the cans of coconut milk and skim the fat from the top of the cans. Discard the remaining coconut water or save for inclusion in smoothies or soups. Scoop two tablespoons of the coconut solids into a microwave-safe dish. Add the chocolate chips to the dish and microwave until melted, about 60–90 seconds. Stir the chocolate chips until smooth, then spread approximately three-quarters of the mixture into the bottom of the pie crust. Set aside the remaining chocolate.

2. Place the remaining coconut solids in a stand mixer and beat until light and fluffy, about 3–4 minutes. Slowly add the almond butter, butter, almond milk, honey, and vanilla to the whipped coconut. Keep whipping the mixture until smooth, light, and fluffy. Spoon the mixture over the chocolate layer in the pie crust. Drizzle the remaining chocolate on top of the pie. Sprinkle with the toasted coconut and almonds. Refrigerate for 1 hour before serving.

Almond Crème Brûlée

Almond milk takes the place of cream in this rich crème brûlée. You don't necessarily need a brûlée torch, but it does make the task of caramelizing the sugar easier. These devices can be purchased online or from specialty kitchen stores.

8 egg yolks
⅓ cup + 4 teaspoons sugar
1 cup unflavored almond milk
1 cup vanilla almond milk

Special Equipment: Four 5-ounce ramekins

1. Preheat the oven to 300°F.
2. In a large bowl, whisk the yolks with ⅓ cup of the sugar for 2 minutes. Add the unflavored and vanilla flavored almond milk to the bowl.
3. Divide the mixture between the four ramekins. Place them in a casserole dish and pour boiling water into the dish so that it reaches halfway up the ramekins. Bake for 40–50 minutes. The center should still jiggle slightly when moved. Remove the ramekins from the oven with tongs and place them on a wire rack to cool completely, and then place them in the refrigerator for 2 hours to chill.
4. Sprinkle 1 teaspoon sugar over the top of each ramekin and caramelize the sugar with a brûlée torch. Or, preheat the broiler to high and place the ramekins on the top rack of the oven, under the heat so that the sugar caramelizes. Keep the door open and watch closely—the sugar will caramelize in about 30–45 seconds. Serve immediately.

MAKES 4 SERVINGS

**PER SERVING
(¼ RECIPE)**

Calories: 269
Calories from Fat: 95
Total Fat: 9.9g, 15%
Saturated Fat: 3.2g, 16%
Total Carb: 18.4g, 6%
Dietary Fiber: 0.5g, 2%
Sugars: 16.8g
Protein: 5.6g
Cholesterol: 420mg, 140%
Sodium: 61mg, 3%

Luscious Lemon Bars

If you grew up loving lemon bars, you can enjoy them even now—without sugar and without flour. The crust of these lemon bars is made with almond flour and almond butter. This flavorful shortbread combo makes you wonder why the original recipe didn't call for these ingredients in the first place. Topped with a zesty lemon custard, these lemon bars are sure to have you feeling like a kid again. Avoiding powdered sugar as part of a paleo diet? Try topping these lemon bars with a sprinkling of lemon zest for a pretty, sugar-free garnish.

1 tablespoon butter

1 cup almond flour

¼ cup almond butter

⅔ cup honey or agave nectar

¼ teaspoon salt

Juice and zest of 8 lemons (about 1 cup juice)

8 eggs

2 tablespoons powdered sugar for dusting (optional)

1. Preheat the oven to 350°F.
2. In a large bowl, use a fork to mix together the butter, almond flour, almond butter, 1 tablespoon of the honey, and salt until a crumbly dough forms. Press into the bottom of an 8 × 8-inch baking dish lined with parchment paper. Bake for 10 minutes.
3. While the crust bakes, whisk together the lemon zest, lemon juice, eggs, and the remaining honey until well mixed. Pour mixture over the hot crust, return to the oven and bake 25–30 minutes more, until the center of the lemon mixture is set. Remove from the oven and let cool. Dust with powdered sugar before slicing into nine squares.

MAKES 9 BARS

**PER SERVING
(1 BAR)**

Calories: 227

Calories from Fat: 97

Total Fat: 10.8g, 17%

Saturated Fat: 2.5g, 13%

Total Carb: 29.5g, 10%

Dietary Fiber: 2.1g, 8%

Sugars: 24.1g

Protein: 7.7g

Cholesterol: 149mg, 50%

Sodium: 133mg, 6%

One-Bite Vanilla Almond Butter Cups

These no-bake almond butter cups are super for Christmas cookie plates and for gratifying your chocolate cravings in a healthier way. The original version, inspired from a recipe in Alicia Silverstone's The Kind Diet, *is made with peanut butter, but I think this almond butter rendition is better. Vanilla bean seeds can be expensive but lend such intense gourmet flavor to this recipe that I couldn't help but add them. However, feel free to substitute 1 teaspoon of pure vanilla extract, if you're feeling particularly happy about having money in the bank, instead of spending it in the baking aisle.*

½ cup butter or Earth Balance
¾ cup almond butter
¾ cup graham cracker crumbs
¼ cup raw honey or maple syrup
Seeds of 1 vanilla bean
1 cup dark chocolate chips (for vegan, must be labeled "dairy-free")
¼ cup coconut milk
¼ cup chopped pecans (optional)

Special Equipment: Muffin tin; cupcake liners

1. Place 12 parchment cupcake liners in a muffin tin. In a microwave-safe bowl, cook butter and almond butter together until melted, about 60–90 seconds. Stir in the graham cracker crumbs, honey, and vanilla bean seeds. Spoon the mixture into the bottom of each cupcake liner.

2. In a small microwave-safe bowl, combine the chocolate chips and coconut milk. Heat in the microwave until the chocolate chips are melted, about 60–90 seconds. Remove from microwave and stir until smooth. Spoon it on top of the almond butter mixture. Top with chopped pecans, if desired.

D
gL
nL
VE
VT

MAKES 12 ALMOND BUTTER CUPS

PER SERVING (1 ALMOND BUTTER CUP)

Calories: 286
Calories from Fat: 202
Total Fat: 22.5g, 35%
Saturated Fat: 8.6g, 43%
Total Carb: 20.2g, 7%
Dietary Fiber: 1.2g, 5%
Sugars: 12.4g
Protein: 4.7g
Cholesterol: 20mg, 7%
Sodium: 102mg, 4%

TIP: Make It for You!

Go Paleo: Swap the graham cracker crumbs for finely shredded coconut. Use honey as the sweetener and add coconut oil instead of butter.

Go Vegan: Use graham cracker crumbs, Earth Balance Butter, and maple syrup or maple sugar. Grain-sweetened, no-dairy chocolate chips will make this recipe totally vegan.

Go Gluten-Free: Gluten-free graham cracker crumbs will keep this recipe celiac-friendly.

TIP: Make It Without the Microwave

Make this recipe in saucepans on the stove, instead of in bowls in the microwave, if preferred.

Three-Ingredient Chocolate-Banana Ice "Cream"

All you need to make creamy, decadent ice cream is a high-speed blender (like a Vitamix) and three easy ingredients. This recipe is a great way to use leftover ripe bananas. Just peel them and put them in a freezer bag for those moments when you just need a frozen treat. Store them in the freezer for up to 1 month. For a rocky-road inspired dessert, top a scoop of this recipe with chopped toasted almonds, chocolate chips, and a dollop of marshmallow cream.

4 ripe bananas, frozen

2 tablespoons roasted almond butter

4 tablespoons unsweetened cocoa

1. Place all the ingredients in a high-speed blender and blend until pureed, about 60 seconds. Use the tamper tool to press the mixture into the blades until pureed. Scoop the mixture straight from the blender and serve.

MAKES 4 SERVINGS

**PER SERVING
(¼ RECIPE)**

Calories: 117

Calories from Fat: 10

Total Fat: 1.1g, 2%

Saturated Fat: 0.6g, 3%

Total Carb: 29.9g, 10%

Dietary Fiber: 4.9g, 19%

Sugars: 14.5g

Protein: 2.4g

Cholesterol: 0mg, 0%

Sodium: 2mg, 0%

METRIC CONVERSIONS

The recipes in this book have not been tested with metric measurements, so some variations might occur.

Remember that the weight of dry ingredients varies according to the volume or density factor: 1 cup of flour weighs far less than 1 cup of sugar, and 1 tablespoon doesn't necessarily hold 3 teaspoons.

GENERAL FORMULAS FOR METRIC CONVERSION

Ounces to grams	→	ounces × 28.35 = grams
Grams to ounces	→	grams × 0.035 = ounces
Pounds to grams	→	pounds × 453.5 = grams
Pounds to kilograms	→	pounds × 0.45 = kilograms
Cups to liters	→	cups ¥ 0.24 = liters
Fahrenheit to Celsius	→	(°F − 32) × 5 ÷ 9 = °C
Celsius to Fahrenheit	→	(°C × 9) ÷ 5 + 32 = °F

LINEAR MEASUREMENTS

½ inch = 1½ cm
1 inch = 2½ cm
6 inches = 15 cm
8 inches = 20 cm
10 inches = 25 cm
12 inches = 30 cm
20 inches = 50 cm

OVEN TEMPERATURE EQUIVALENTS, FAHRENHEIT (F) AND CELSIUS (C)

100°F = 38°C
200°F = 95°C
250°F = 120°C
300°F = 150°C
350°F = 180°C
400°F = 205°C
450°F = 230°C

WEIGHT (MASS) MEASUREMENTS

1 ounce = 30 grams
2 ounces = 55 grams
3 ounces = 85 grams
4 ounces = ¼ pound = 125 grams
8 ounces = ½ pound = 240 grams
12 ounces = ¾ pound = 375 grams
16 ounces = 1 pound = 454 grams

VOLUME (DRY) MEASUREMENTS

¼ teaspoon = 1 milliliter
½ teaspoon = 2 milliliters
¾ teaspoon = 4 milliliters
1 teaspoon = 5 milliliters
1 tablespoon = 15 milliliters
¼ cup = 59 milliliters
⅓ cup = 79 milliliters
½ cup = 118 milliliters
⅔ cup = 158 milliliters
¾ cup = 177 milliliters
1 cup = 225 milliliters
4 cups or 1 quart = 1 liter
½ gallon = 2 liters
1 gallon = 4 liters

VOLUME (LIQUID) MEASUREMENTS

1 teaspoon = ⅙ fluid ounce = 5 milliliters
1 tablespoon = ½ fluid ounce = 15 milliliters
2 tablespoons = 1 fluid ounce = 30 milliliters
¼ cup = 2 fluid ounces = 60 milliliters
⅓ cup = 2⅔ fluid ounces = 79 milliliters
½ cup = 4 fluid ounces = 118 milliliters
1 cup or ½ pint = 8 fluid ounces = 250 milliliters
2 cups or 1 pint = 16 fluid ounces = 500 milliliters
4 cups or 1 quart = 32 fluid ounces = 1,000 milliliters
1 gallon = 4 liters

THE BEST ALMONDS OF THE BUNCH

The almond-based product market is growing quickly. With fresh offerings arriving frequently on store shelves, we as consumers are left wondering if we should try the new, or stay with the tried-and-true. From raw almond butter to almond-coconut milk and from organic to gourmet, almond products now come in a dazzling range of options.

Several large companies have emerged as leaders in the almond-product marketplace, but smaller niche companies are starting to churn out beautiful options that will lend flavor, texture, and fun to your cooking. Which of these products are worth your penny? Here are a few of the options currently available online and in grocery stores and a review of their costs, flavors, and best uses to help you navigate the growing list of almond butter, almond milk, and almond flour products.

Almond Butter

Justin's Almond Butter
Ingredients: Dry roasted almonds, organic palm fruit oil
Calories: 200 per 2 tablespoons
Made with dry roasted almonds, this almond butter might need a slight stir right out of the jar but otherwise has a rich roasted almond flavor and nice consistency, making it a good fit for sweet and savory recipes. Justin's uses palm fruit oil to minimize oil separation in their nut butters, and it contains no trans-fatty acids.

Justin's Honey Almond Butter
Ingredients: Dry roasted almonds, honey powder (sugar, honey), organic palm fruit oil, sea salt
Calories: 190 per 2 tablespoons

Justin's Honey Almond Butter is sweet and easy to spread; it's a good almond butter for most of the dessert recipes in this book. Note the ingredients list includes sugar and honey, so vegans or sugar-free foodies will want to stick with raw butters from other brands.

Justin's Maple Almond Butter

Ingredients: Dry roasted almonds, maple sugar, organic palm fruit oil, sea salt
Calories: 90 per 14-gram pouch
Made with natural products and minimal processing, the Justin's brand of almond butters may be the easiest to find on store shelves. Justin's Maple Almond Butter is made with dry roasted almonds, maple sugar, organic palm fruit oil, and sea salt. A short list of ingredients, though take note that this variety of Justin's almond butter is made with roasted almonds and includes sugar. So, raw foodies and those avoiding sugar will want to turn to other brands. This Justin's flavor is mildly sweet, with the finest and most enjoyable little crunch of sugar crystals. The consistency is smooth and spreadable. Ideal for sweeter recipes like cookies or fruit dips, keep in mind that any sugar called for in the recipe list can be cut down slightly because of the sugar content in the almond butter itself.

Justin's Vanilla Almond Butter

Ingredients: Dry roasted almonds, organic cane sugar, organic cocoa butter, vanilla, palm fruit oil, sea salt

Calories: 180 per 2 tablespoons
While almond butter and vanilla sounds like a perfect mix, this mildly sweet Justin's flavor is my least favorite. It has an odd sort of aftertaste, and isn't recommended for eating raw, but would work well for dessert recipes like cookies.

MaraNatha All Natural No Stir Almond Butter, Crunchy

Ingredients: Dry roasted almonds, organic unrefined cane sugar, palm oil, sea salt

Calories: 190 per 2 tablespoons
Roasted almonds are double-ground to create an extremely smooth base with the crunch of larger almond pieces added for texture. Roasted almonds result in a deeper, richer flavor, which pairs nicely with savory cooking. Available in most grocery stores, this almond butter is a good place to start if you've never tried almond butter before.

MaraNatha All Natural No Stir Raw Maple Almond Butter, Creamy

Ingredients: Raw almonds, maple sugar, palm oil, sea salt
Calories: 180 per 2 tablespoons
Slightly sweet with the fine crunch of maple sugar granules and finely chopped almond bits, this almond butter is ready right out of the jar, no stirring needed. Though it's technically a creamy version, there is a slight crunch and chew with each bite. The texture is a little runny; it will sit on a spoon in a heap, but turn the spoon

over and the almond butter will lose a bit of its form. Soft enough for spreading, perfect for cooking and baking. This is a mild, thick almond butter that holds up well to a variety of preparations.

MaraNatha No-Stir Coconut Almond Butter
Ingredients: Dry roasted almonds, creamed coconut, evaporated cane syrup, palm oil, salt
Calories: 190 per 2 tablespoons
This is a firm, smooth, slightly sweet almond butter with a mild coconut flavor and a thin layer of oil on top. Perfect for baking because of the natural almond oils with the addition of palm oil, this nut butter works into batters well and yields baked goods that are kissed with the flavor of almonds and a hint of coconut.

MaraNatha Organic Raw Almond Butter, creamy
Ingredients: Organic raw almonds
Calories: 180 per 2 tablespoons
To be considered raw, food products must not be exposed to temperatures over 104–120°F. Many diets, including raw vegan and paleo diets promote the benefits of raw versus roasted nuts because high cooking temperatures can kill enzymes, vitamins, and nutrients in fresh foods. For a truly clean eating experience, MaraNatha Organic Raw Almond Butter is as basic as nut butters get, as it contains only one ingredient, organic raw almonds, making it, as MaraNatha proclaims, "the next best thing to eating your almonds straight from the orchard." The texture of this nut butter is quite runny, and it settles under a 1/2-inch layer of oil at the top of the jar; be sure to stir before spreading. To get the full benefits of this nut butter, use it only in recipes that require no cooking.

NuttZo Seven Seed Nut & Butter, Original
Ingredients: Organic peanuts, organic cashews, organic almonds, organic Brazil nuts, organic sunflower seeds, organic flax seeds, organic hazelnuts, sea salt
Calories: 180 per 2 tablespoons
Thick and creamy with the mixed flavor of a variety of nuts including peanuts, cashews, and almonds, this creamy butter is perfect for the passionate nut-lover, though less-enthusiastic nut eaters may find it *too* nutty. Try using this butter as a spread or add it to a fruit dip. This one pairs better with savory recipes, because the peanuts and Brazil nuts lend a unique flavor that might add an off-taste to baked goods.

365 Almond Butter, Creamy
Ingredients: Dry roasted almonds
Calories: 180 per 2 tablespoons
The store brand for Whole Foods Market, this almond butter tends to cost less in the store than other name brands. A thin layer of oil sits on top. Once stirred into the jar, the resulting texture is smooth and nicely pureed. Very creamy and uniform, perfect for cooking, baking, and spreading.

Other online brands worth putting in your pantry:

- Almondie Almond Butter (http://www.almondie.com)
- Once Again Raw Almond Butter (https://www.onceagainnutbutter.com/)
- Wild Friends Vanilla Espresso Almond Butter (http://www.wildfriendsfoods.com/)

Almond Flour

Almond flour can be hard to locate, unless you know where to look. Most grocers carry expensive little bags of almond meal from Bob's Red Mill, which works beautifully for crumbles or breadcrumb substitutes but tends to be less successful in baked goods like cookies and quick breads.

To get the finest ground almond flour and the biggest bang for your buck, it's highly recommended that you purchase almond flour in bulk online. Purchased by the pound, almond flour will run about $8–9. However, the cost per pound is generally as low as $5 when purchased in 25-pound bags.

Since good almond flour is basically the same—made from blanched almonds and finely ground—rather than offering reviews of individual brands, here's a basic list of products currently on the market that are worth keeping in your kitchen. Each of these almond flours is well ground, works great in the recipes included in this book, and is easily ordered from companies with a known track record.

Benefit Your Life Market & Bakery
Product: Organic blanched almond flour
Where to buy: www.benefityourlifestore.com
Cost: About $15 for a 1.5 pound bag

Digestive Wellness
Product: Super-fine almond flour (kosher)
Where to buy: www.digestivewellness.com
Cost: About $9 for a 1-pound bag

Honeyville Farms
Product: Blanched almond flour
Where to buy: www.honeyvillegrain.com
Cost: About $40 for a 5-pound bag

JK Gourmet Grain-Free
Product: Super finely ground blanched almond flour
Where to buy: www.jkgourmet.com
Cost: About $22 for a 2-pound bag

Nuts.com
Product: Blanched almond flour
Where to buy: www.nuts.com
Cost: About $8 for a 1-pound bag

Almond Milk

With several almond milk products on the market, it can be tricky knowing which brand, flavor, and company is worth your hard-earned dollar. With shelf-stable almond milk options (typically found in the pantry aisles of most grocery stores) and refrigerated almond milk options (in flavors from "original" to "unsweetened" to vanilla and chocolate), which brands deliver the best quality, taste, and texture? And which work best for drinking, or cooking, or baking? Here are a few varieties of the more common brands available in most U.S. stores, with some basic notes about texture, flavor, and additives. The hope is not to steer you in any one direction but to give you an overview of each product, so you can cut straight to the chase and buy the best almond milk for your needs.

Blue Diamond Almond Breeze, refrigerated

Flavors: Original, Original Unsweetened, Chocolate, Vanilla, Vanilla Unsweetened

Balanced and mild, with a consistency most similar to cow's milk (the chocolate and vanilla almond milks seem to pour slightly thicker), Almond Breeze products may be some of the easiest to locate in the United States since they're carried in most major grocery stores. Many almond milk products can have an undesirable thickness, but the texture of Almond Breeze (especially the unsweetened varieties) almond milks is smooth, desirably thinner than other brands, and with little or no almond flavor at all. Very bright and fresh tasting. Several of the flavors uses food-grade carageenan—a seaweed-based food additive—to thicken and stabilize the product for shipping and storage. The unsweetened varieties contain no sugar or cane juice. The products are made in a peanut-free facility, from non-GMO almonds. The unsweetened and original almond milks work well in savory recipes or as a substitute for cow's milk. The vanilla and chocolate varieties make a great addition to coffee, milkshakes, and other sweet treats.

Blue Diamond Almond Breeze, shelf stable

Flavors: Original, Original Unsweetened, Vanilla, Vanilla Unsweetened, Chocolate, Chocolate Unsweetened

Available in the pantry section of most major grocers and health-food stores, the shelf-stable Almond Breeze is creamy with a consistency and taste nearly equivalent to the refrigerated brands. The milks are vegan, kosher, and completely dairy-free. A perfect way to keep a tasty dairy alternative ever available on the shelves of your pantry and a great option to pack for camping and road trips as well. For cooking and baking, the original unsweetened and vanilla unsweetened almond milks are best. They contain no added sugar or cane juice and mix well into quick bread, waffles, and biscuit recipes. It's not recommended that these products be added to packaged pudding products.

Pacific Organic Almond Milk

Products: Almond Original, Almond Vanilla, Almond Original Unsweetened, Almond Vanilla Unsweetened, Organic Almond Chocolate

You'll find this brand of almond milk in the shelf-stable section of most whole food and natural food stores. It's certified organic, so health-conscious eaters focusing on clean eating will find this brand worth hunting down. The texture of the unsweetened varieties is thin with little almond flavor. The chocolate versions come in single serving packs and have a consistency similar to other shelf-stable chocolate beverages, which may be desired by some sippers but snubbed by those who are fussy about texture. If organic food is a priority, Pacific Organic Almond Milk is a good alternative for drinking, but the texture is thin and not preferred in cooking or baking. You're not going to ruin any recipe by using it, but add it slowly to soups and sauces to keep from overthinning your final dish.

Silk PureAlmond

Flavors: Vanilla, Original, Unsweetened Vanilla, Unsweetened Original, Light Vanilla, Light Original, Dark Chocolate

Silk almond milk is dairy free, soy free, gluten free, lactose free, cholesterol free, egg free, and MSG free. Most of the flavors have a short list of ingredients and additives (the original contains filtered water, almonds, cane sugar, sea salt, locust bean gum, sunflower lecithin, gellan gum, and added vitamins and minerals like calcium carbonate and vitamin E acetate among others.) The texture is slightly thicker than cow's milk, though it's smooth and creamy when poured. This makes it ideal for pouring over oatmeal or blending into smoothies and shakes. For cooking and baking, the unsweetened and unsweetened original recipes are recommended.

So Delicious Almond Milk

Products: Original Almond Plus 5x Protein, Almond Plus Unsweetened 5x Protein, Vanilla Almond Plus 5x Protein

Certified gluten free and dairy free, So Delicious almond milk products boast five times the protein of other leading almond milk brands. The flavor is thicker and chalkier than some newbie almond milk drinkers may find palatable, but the boosted protein makes this almond milk a good mix-in for lattes and smoothies.

ACKNOWLEDGMENTS

Compiling a cookbook of 150+ new recipes is no small task. It takes time, it takes a lot of taste testing, and it takes a team of truly supportive and talented friends and experts to pull it all together. I can't claim a single ounce of credit for this book without also giving props to people who have helped all along the way.

To Launie Kettler of TeenyTinyKitchen.com, for editing recipes, bouncing ideas, and helping me push the bounds of the recipes I make up in my head. Thank you, darling girl, for a keen eye, happy emailage, and the finest set of podcast recommendations ever. You really are my Gus.

To Melanie North (http://www.melanienorthphotography.com/) for buying props, talking shop, and squeezing me into her schedule, even as her husband battled (and won! You go guys!) cancer. Mel, thank you for your artistic eye, your recipe testing, and your feisty willingness to jump in and help me with the ropes.

To Franklin Bennett (http://Impressionswest.photoshelter.com) for Saturday afternoons, standing in my kitchen as we drizzled hollandaise over eggs, placed single stems of tarragon, and followed the light. Thank you, dearest, for keeping me raw.

To Dalyn Miller of Hollanpub.com, and the lovely Miss Holly Schmidt. Thank you for a brilliant idea, absurd amounts of emotional support and cheerleading, and for believing in me to begin with. You've rocked my world and I'm grateful beyond words.

To Renee Sedaliar. For being the cheeriest, most thoughtful editor ever. You've found the perfect balance between checking in and offering creative space, and I'm so grateful for your impeccable ability to do both.

Source Materials

Stats on rising almond product specialty market from http://www.almondboard.com

INDEX

B

Bacon
  Almond Butter Breakfast
    Sandwiches, 42
  Almond Grilled Elvis, 110
  Almond Toast, 43
  Bacon-Onion Corn Muffins, 61
  McMuffin Morning Munchers,
    41
  Melty Bacon-Almond Crostini,
    97
  Open-Faced Almond Butter and
    Bacon Sammy, 109
  as waffle topping, 37
Bagel, Spicy Brie, 121
Baked Vanilla Donuts with
  Chocolate Frosting, 186–187
Baking, with almond flour, 2
Baking powder, using almond flour
  and adjusting amount of, 6
Bananas
  Almond Butter Muffins, 62
  Almond Grilled Elvis, 110
  Banana Almond Bread, 65
  Banana Almond Butter Protein
    Blast, 85
  Banana Bread Oatmeal, 39
  Banana Cream Pie, 197
  Chocolate Almond Smoothie,
    83
  McMuffin Morning Munchers,
    41
  Open-Faced Almond Butter and
    Banana Sandwiches, 108
  Paleo Almond Butter Banana
    Pancakes, 32
  Three-Ingredient Chocolate-
    Banana Ice "Cream," 204
  as topping for waffles, 37

Bare-Bones Raw Almond Butter,
  22
Basic Almond Flour, 26
Basic Berry Waffles, 35
Basil, Almond Butter Pesto, 158
Bean sprouts
  Fried Chickpea Salad, 163
  Thai Curry Chicken Noodle
    Soup, 134–135
Beef
  Almond Butter Browned Steak,
    154
  Korean Lettuce Wraps, 172–173
  Primal Power Meatballs, 151
  Steak Salad with Tomatoes,
    Scallions, and Ginger-Almond
    Vinaigrette, 166
Belgian Sweet Waffles, 36–37
Bella mushrooms, Creamy Dreamy
  Stroganoff, 155
Berry Syrup, 33
Beverages, 73–87
  ABC Protein Shake, 82
  Almond Butter Hot Chocolate,
    79
  Almond Café Latte, 74
  Almond Milk Cappuccino, 74
  Almond White Marshmallow Hot
    Cocoa, 78
  Chai Latte, 75
  coffees, 74–75
  Double Dark Hot Cocoa, 77
  Mocha, 74
  Orange Almond Whippy, 81
  Peppermint-Chocolate Mocha,
    80
  Pumpkin Spice Latte, 75
  Vanilla Almond Steamer, 76
  See also Smoothies

Grapes, red
  Almond Butter Chicken Salad, 123
  Creamy Cauliflower Soup, 130
Grapeseed oil, 8, 9, 12
Grass-fed butter, 9
Gravy, Creamy Pepper, 102
Great Northern beans, White Bean and Roasted Red Pepper Spread, 95
Greek yogurt, Creamy Almond Butter and Honey Apple Dip, 93
Grilled Cheese Croutons, 127
Grilled Cheese Sandwiches
  Almond-Crusted Pesto, 122
  Thai-Style, 116–117
Grilled Chicken Sandwich, 120
Grok's Chicken Fingers, 140

H
Ham, Enlightened Monte Cristo, 119
Hand-held blender, 11
Hanger steak, Steak Salad with Tomatoes, Scallions, and Ginger-Almond Vinaigrette, 166
Heart disease, almonds and reduction in, 1, 2
Herbed Tomato Salsa, 128–129
High-speed, industrial-strength blender, 11
Himalayan pink salt, 10
Honey, raw, 9
Honey Almond Crunch Crackers, 91
Honeyed Vanilla Almond Butter, 24

Hot Cocoa
  Almond Butter Hot Chocolate, 79
  Almond White Marshmallow, 78
  Double Dark Hot Cocoa, 77
Hummus, Almond Butter, 92

I
Ice "Cream," Three-Ingredient Chocolate-Banana, 204
Iron, in almonds, 2

J
Jalapeño-Cheddar Corn Muffins, 61

K
Kale
  Coconut-Almond Green Smoothie, 87
  Marinated Spicy Kale Salad, 105
  Roasted Cinnamon Squash, 104
Key Lime Cream Pie, 197
The Kind Diet (Silverstone), 202
Kitchen equipment, 11–12
Korean Lettuce Wraps, 172–173
Kosher salt, 10

L
Lactose intolerance, almond milk and, 3
Lacy Almond Crepes, 30–31
Lattes
  Almond Café, 74
  Chai, 75
  Pumpkin Spice, 75
Lazy Day Udon Noodles, 159
Lectin, 2
Leeks, Velvet Almond Soup, 136

ABOUT THE AUTHOR

Brooke McLay is freelance food writer, food photographer, and recipe developer for Betty Crocker, Good Cook, General Mills, Tablespoon.com, and Disney's Babble. As the co-host of online food and décor video series, HisXHers.com, Brooke brings her buoyant, feisty passion for food and family to life. She has also hosted cooking shorts with Bisquick, Pillsbury, and Chef Mom. She shares her original healthy recipes and writes about her own attempts to transition her family from a traditional Western diet, to plant-based and paleo-friendly foods on her website, CheekyKitchen.com